FOOTBALL
KIT DESIGNER
COLOURING BOOK
FOR KIDS

THIS BOOK BELONGS TO

_ _

_ _

Copyright © 2024. All rights reserved.
This book or any portion thereof may not be reproduced or used in any manner whatsoever without express written permission of the publisher

WELCOME TO YOUR ULTIMATE FOOTBALL ADVENTURE!

Welcome to the world where YOU are the football manager, designer, and superstar! Whether you've always dreamed of building the best football team on the planet or crafting the coolest kits ever seen, this book is your ticket to football glory!

This book is divided into three fun sections, each packed with different activities to fuel your football creativity

Start your adventure in **Section 1: Create Your Own Football Team**, where you'll name your team, design a standout logo, and choose your winning formation. Everything is up to you!

In **Section 2: Design Your Own Football Kit**, take on the role of kit designer. Color and customize jerseys, boots, and gloves with awesome patterns, while learning amazing football facts along the way!

Finally, unleash your creativity in **Section 3: Design Your Own Football Kit with Blank Templates**. Invent your own patterns, mix colors, and create a kit that's truly unique—each page comes with a cool football fact to inspire you.

Are you ready? Grab your colors and let's kick off this ultimate football adventure

The pitch is yours!

SECTION 1: CREATE YOUR OWN FOOTBALL TEAM

Welcome to the heart of your football adventure! In this section, you'll build your dream team from scratch. From naming your team and designing the perfect kit, to picking your star player and creating an unbeatable strategy, every decision is in your hands. You'll even get to scout your rival team, design game tickets, and create a chant that will echo through the stadium. With each step, you're not just creating a team—you're bringing a football legend to life. And if you think of something extra, we've included space for you to add your own unique steps. Get ready to lead your team to glory!

STEP 1: NAME YOUR TEAM & DESIGN THE BADGE

Your team needs an awesome name and a cool badge to stand out! Think of a name that's strong, fun, or totally unique, then create a badge that shows off your team's style. Let's make your team unforgettable!

Team NAME

Team BADGE

STEP 2: DESIGN YOUR TEAM KIT

It's time to suit up your team for the big game! In this step, you'll create the complete team kit, from the jersey and shorts to the boots, goalkeeper gloves, and socks. Design a look that's bold, unique, and ready to impress on the pitch.

Get ready to make your team the best-dressed and most intimidating on the field!

Jersey Design

Shorts Design

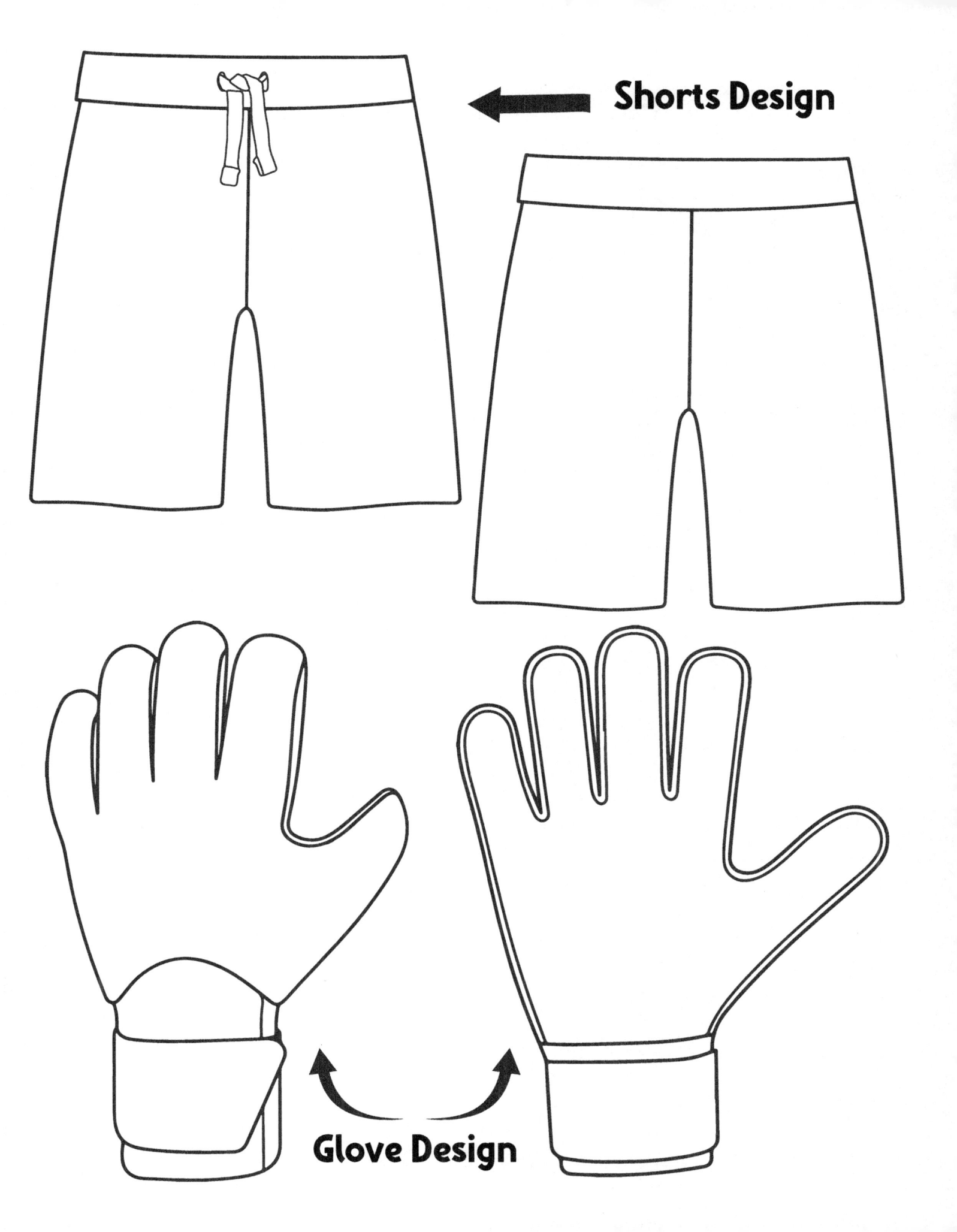

Glove Design

Boots Design

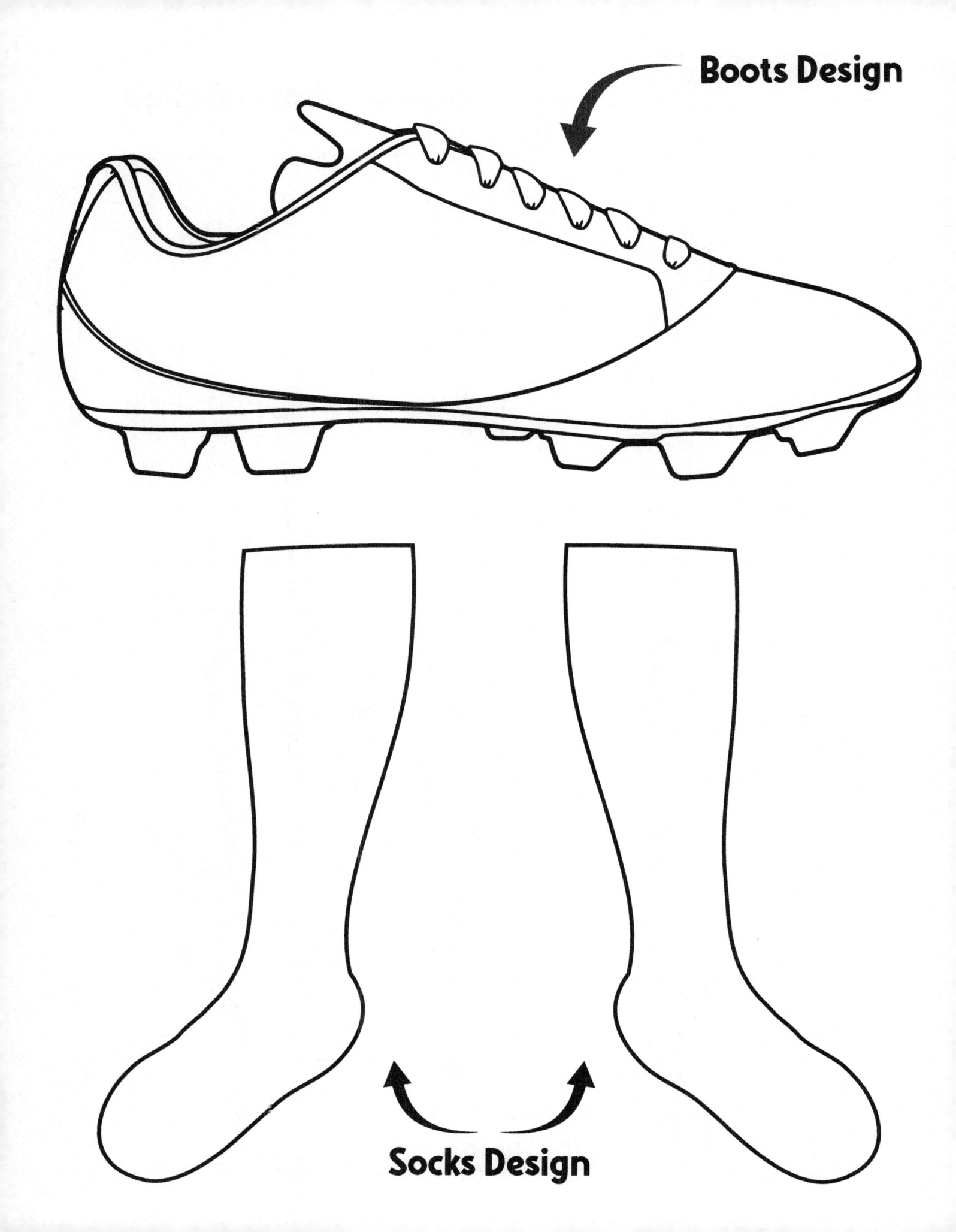

Socks Design

STEP 3: DEFINE YOUR TEAM'S PHILOSOPHY

What makes your team special? In this step, you'll decide the core values that will guide your players on and off the pitch. Whether it's being ambitious, inspiring, connected, or fair, write down the values that will define your team's spirit and identity.

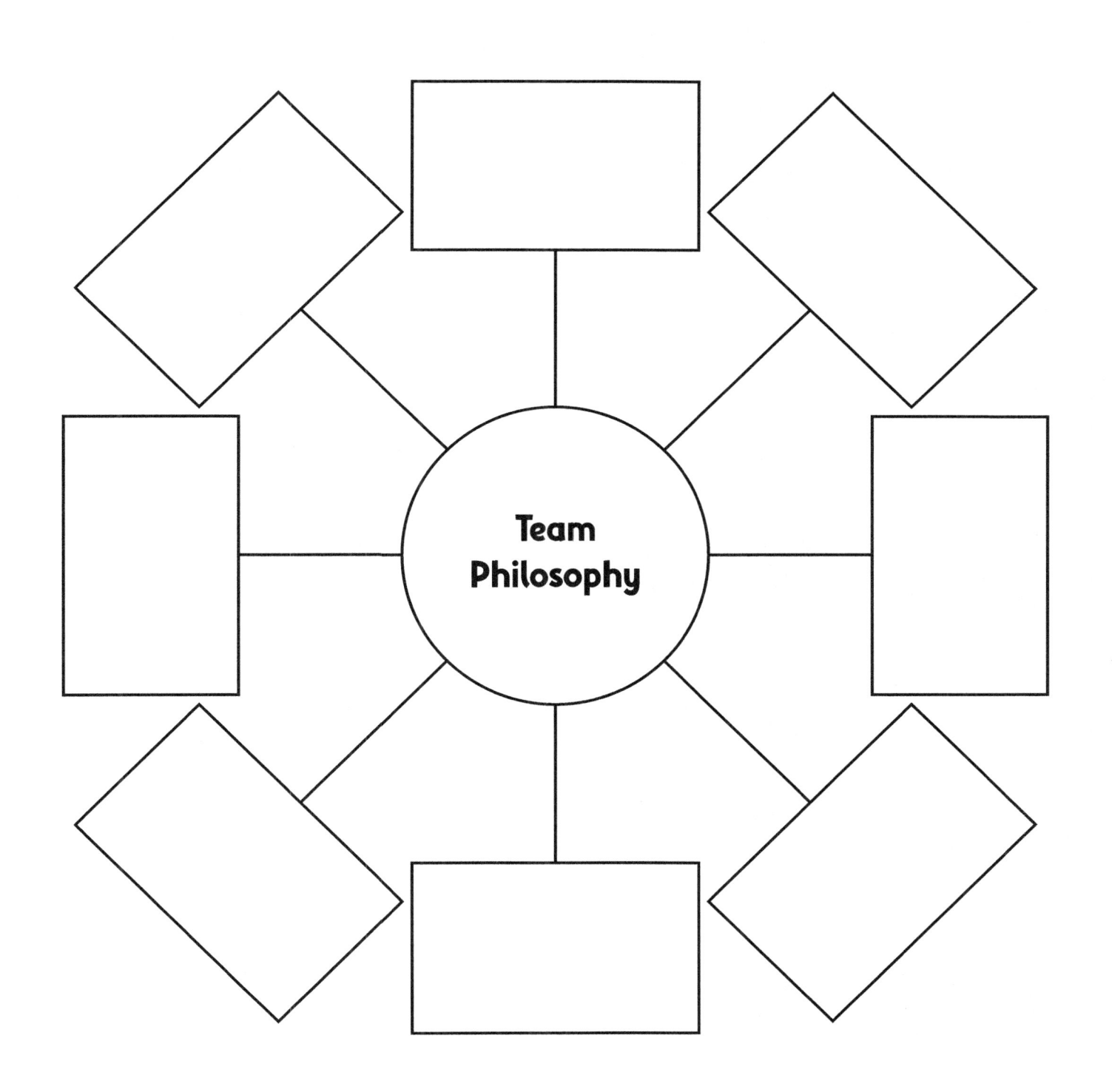

Team Philosophy

STEP 4: SQUAD LIST

Every great team needs star players—and a brilliant manager! In this step, you'll choose 26 players for your dream team, plus a manager to lead them. Pick current stars, legendary players, or your all-time favorites.

The manager can be anyone from today, a legendary coach from the past, or even you! Write down your players' names, positions, jersey numbers, and choose a manager who'll guide your unbeatable team to victory!

Name	Position	Jersey Number

Team Manager

STEP 5: PICK YOUR STAR PLAYER

Every dream team needs a superstar! In this step, you'll choose one player from your squad who you believe has what it takes to be the best in the world. This player is destined to win the Ballon d'Or! Fill in the Player Profile Card with all the details about your star—show the world why they're the greatest!

Name: _____

Position: _____

Jersey number: _____

Country: _____

Height: _____

Weight: _____

Age: _____

Nickname: _____

Preferred Foot (R/L/Both): _____

Favorite Move/Skill: _____

Image

Strengths:
(List the player's top strengths, like speed, dribbling, passing, etc.)

_____
_____
_____
_____

Achievements:
(List any major trophies, awards, or records the player has won)

_____
_____
_____
_____

Why They're the Best:
(Write a few sentences about why this player is the best in the world)

_____
_____
_____
_____

Fun Fact About the Player:
(Add a fun or interesting fact about your star player)

_____
_____
_____
_____

STEP 6: PLAN YOUR STRATEGY & SET YOUR FORMATION

Start by crafting your team's winning strategy! Think about how your players will work together to outsmart the competition. Will you focus on a strong defense, swift counter-attacks, or creative playmaking? Once you've got your strategy down, position your players on the pitch and choose the formation that will bring your team to victory!

Attacking Style: How will your team score? Fast counter-attacks or passing for the perfect chance?

_____
_____
_____
_____

Defensive Approach: What's your strategy for defense? Stay back or press high to win the ball early?

_____
_____
_____
_____

Star Player Role: What's your star player's role? Scoring goals or setting up chances?

_____
_____
_____
_____

Captain's Influence: Who will be the captain? What makes them a great leader, and how will they inspire the team?

_____
_____
_____

Game-Changing Moments: If the game is tied late, what's your strategy?

_____
_____
_____
_____

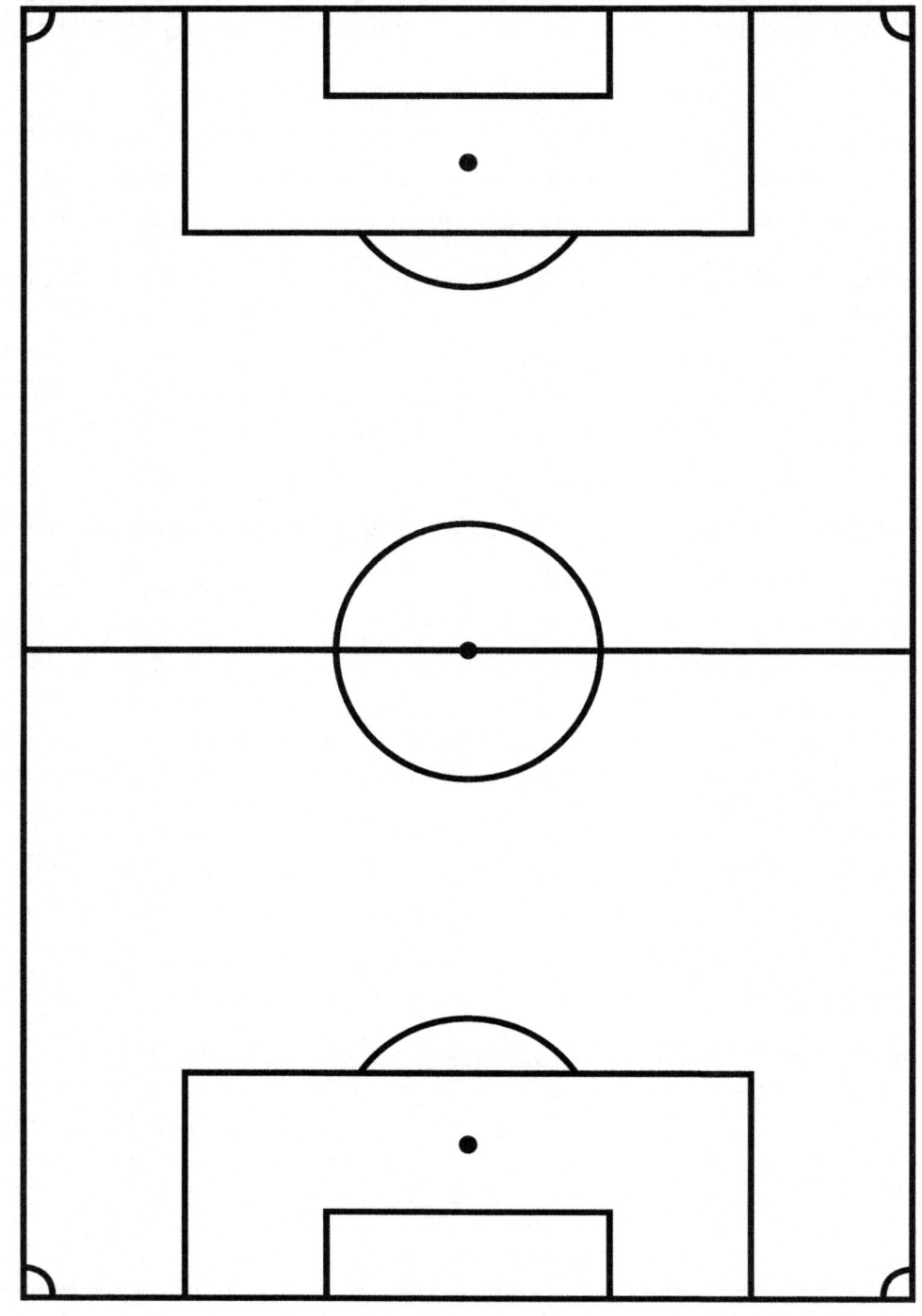

Special Tactics: Any secret tactics or moves to surprise the opponents? How will you use them?
_____
_____
_____
_____
_____
_____
_____
_____

STEP 7: DESIGN YOUR TEAM'S HOME STADIUM

Every great team needs an epic home stadium! In this step, you'll create the ultimate arena for your team to play in. Use the football pitch template and draw the stadium around it, and check out the image for inspiration. Will it have towering stands, cool decorations, or even a rooftop? Make it a place where your fans will cheer their hearts out!

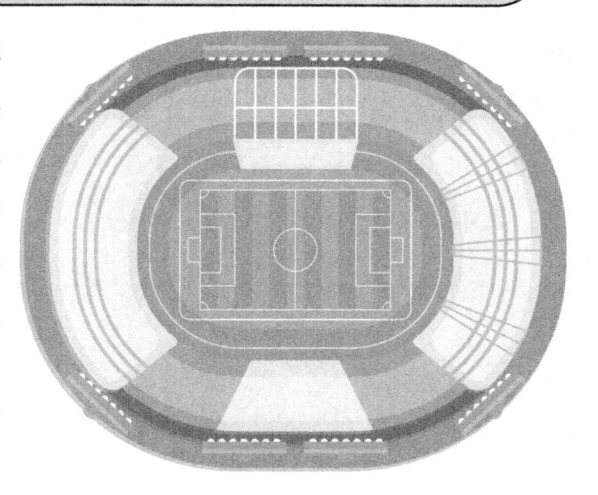

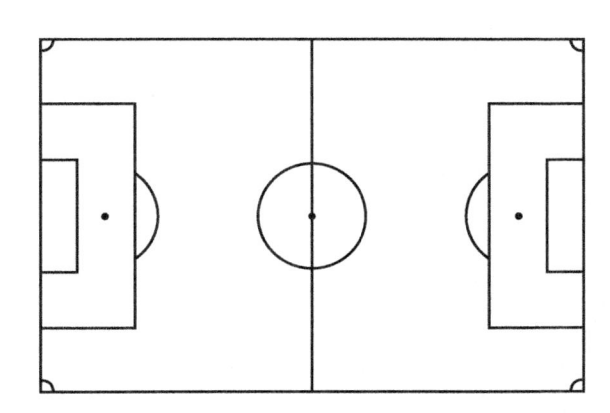

STEP 8: DRAW YOUR TEAM'S MASCOT

Give your team a mascot that will pump up the crowd and bring good luck. Draw an animal, character, or symbol that represents your team's spirit and strength. Your mascot can appear on your team's badge, kit, or even in your fans' chants!

Name of Mascot:

_____

How does it bring good luck?

_____
_____
_____
_____
_____
_____

my favorite part of my design is:

_____
_____
_____
because _____
_____
_____
_____
_____
_____
_____

STEP 9: DESIGN YOUR TEAM'S FOOTBALL

Every team needs a unique football to match their style! In this step, you'll design two different variations of your team's official ball. Use the templates to draw your designs—whether you go for bold patterns, cool colors, or something completely original, make sure your football stands out on the pitch!

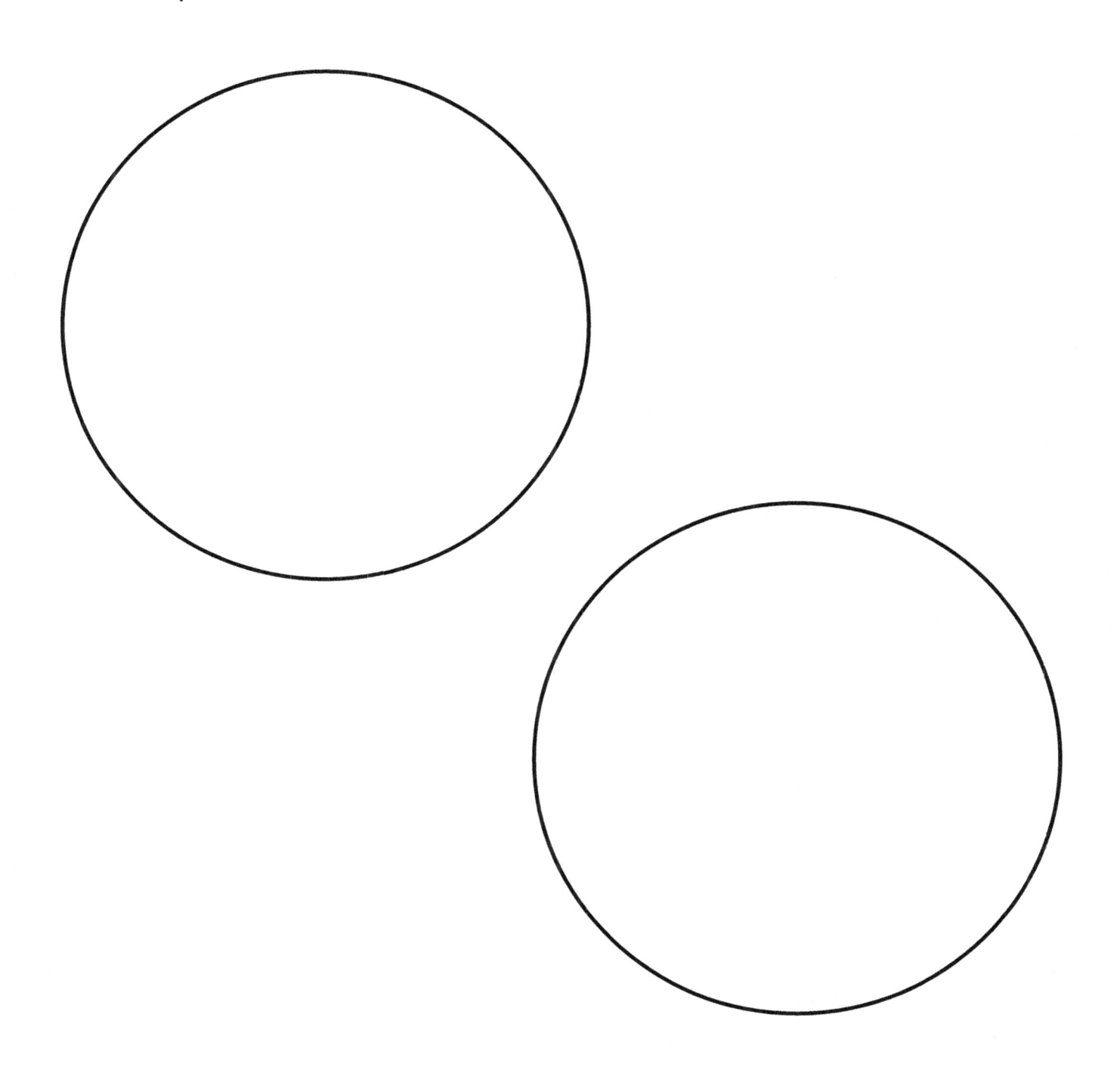

STEP 10: CREATE YOUR TEAM'S GAME TICKETS

It's time to get fans excited for your team's matches! In this step, you'll design tickets for your team's games using the templates provided. Add your own flair with colors, logos, and special details that will make every ticket a collector's item for your fans!

STEP 11: SCOUT YOUR RIVAL TEAM

Every great team needs a worthy adversary! In this step, you'll research a team in the current league that you think will be your biggest competition. Find out what makes them strong, who their key players are, and how your team can outplay them on the field and secure the league title!

Team Information

Team Name: _____

Nickname: _____

Location: _____

Home Stadium: _____

Manager
(Who is the manager, and what is their style of play?)

_____
_____
_____
_____

Top Players
(Who are the standout stars on this team?)

_____
_____
_____
_____
_____
_____

Strengths
(What are the team's biggest strengths?)

_____
_____
_____
_____
_____
_____

Weaknesses
(Where could your team find opportunities to beat them?)

_____
_____
_____

Game Plan
(Develop a plan to outplay your rival. Consider strategies, tactics, and player matchups)

_____
_____
_____

STEP 12: CREATE YOUR TEAM'S CHANT

Every great team has a chant that their fans shout from the stands. Create a catchy chant for your team that the fans can sing to cheer them on during matches. Make it fun and full of energy!

STEP 13: DESIGN YOUR FANS HEADBAND

Every fan needs the perfect gear to show their team spirit! In this step, you'll design a headband for your fans to wear during matches. Use the template to create a headband that's bold, colorful, and full of team pride. Make sure your fans stand out in the crowd!

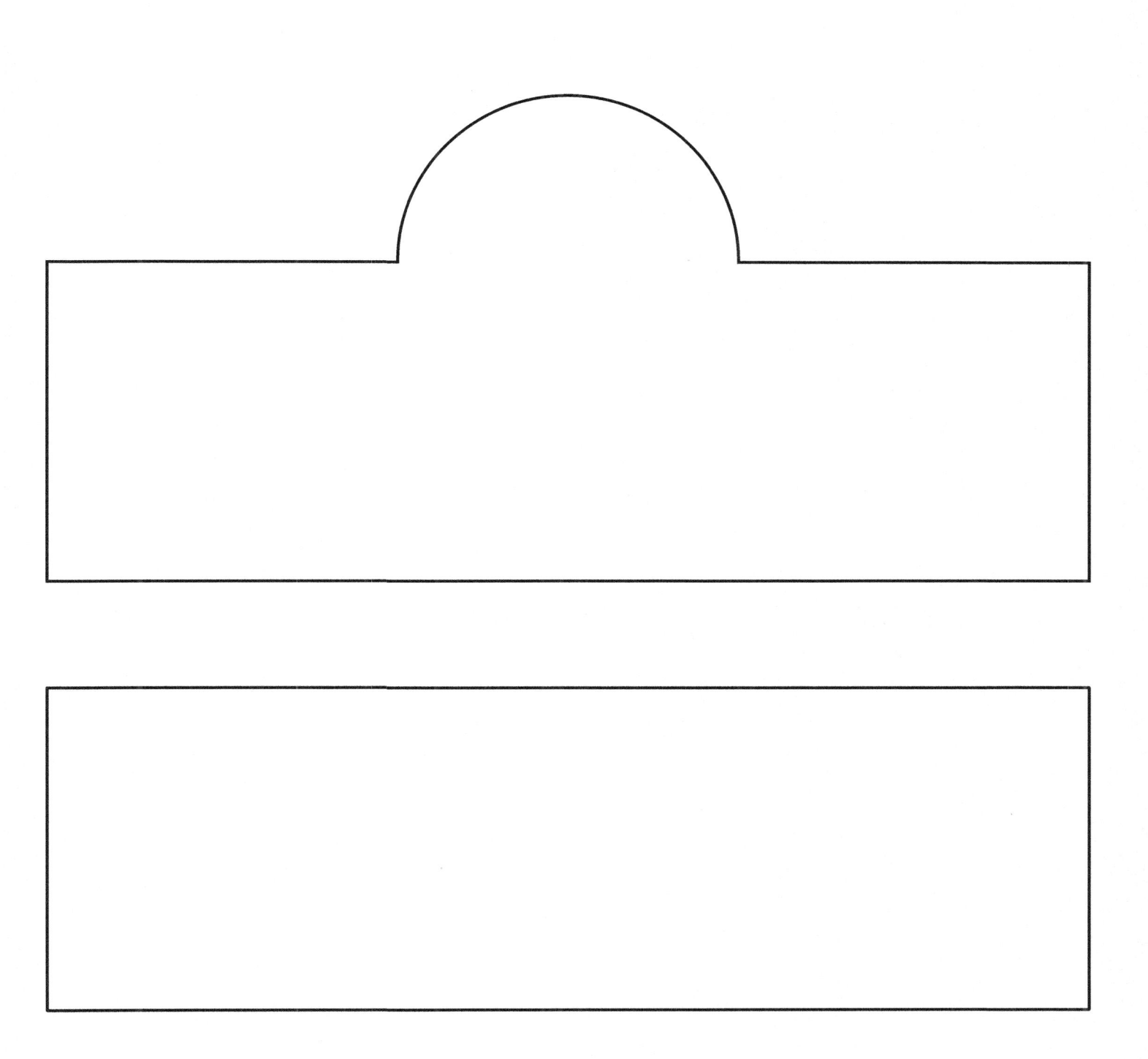

SECTION 2: DESIGN YOUR OWN FOOTBALL KIT

Now it's time to unleash your creativity and design the coolest football kits ever! In this section, you can customize jerseys, boots, and gloves to your heart's content. Experiment with colors, styles, and patterns to bring your unique vision to life. Plus, discover fascinating football facts that will fuel your creativity and keep you inspired as you design your dream kit.

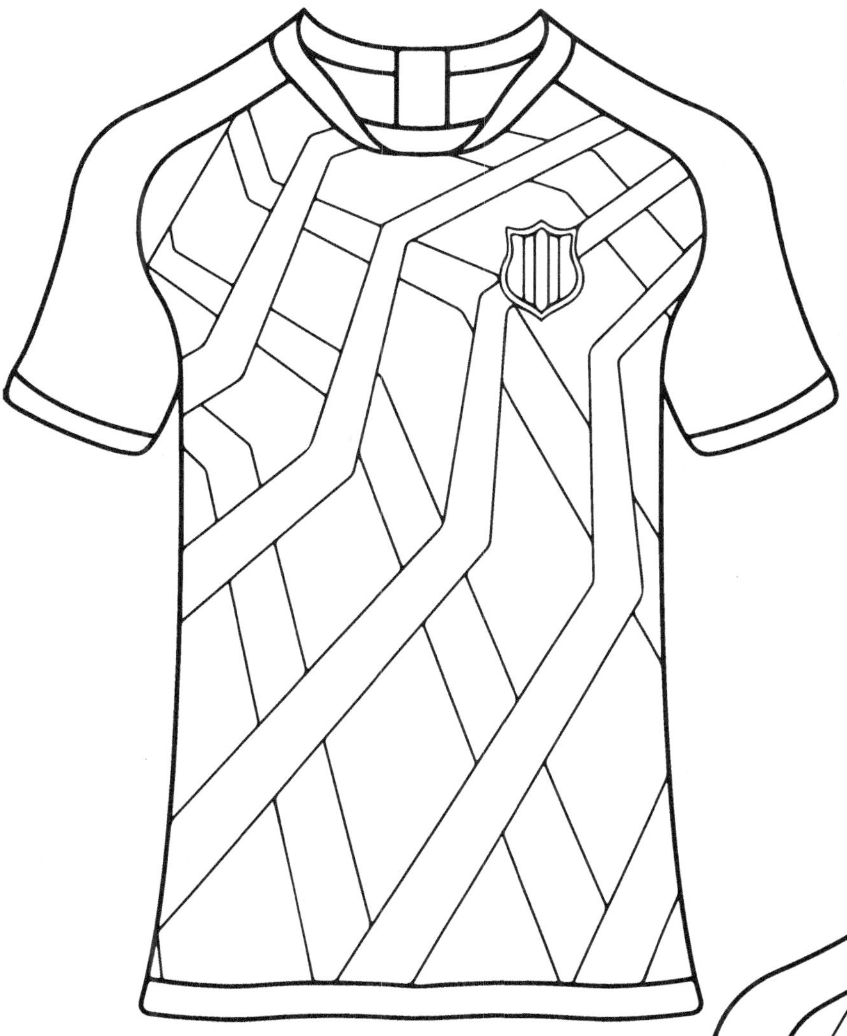

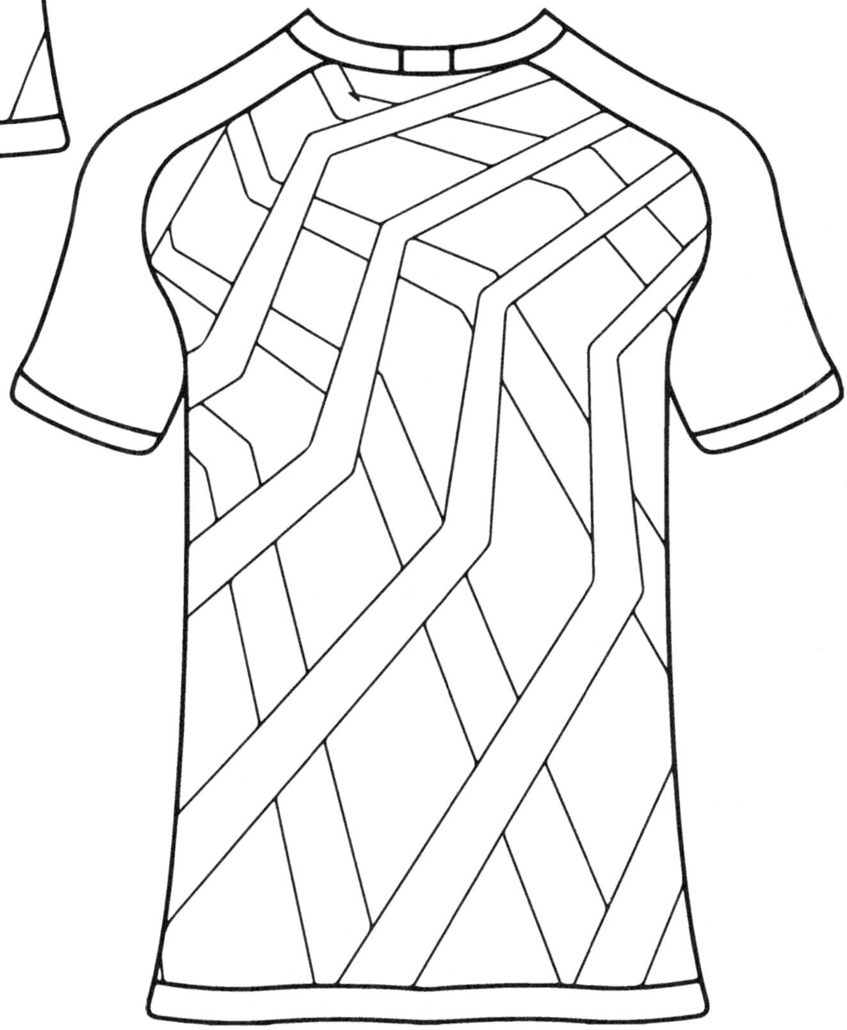

DID YOU KNOW!!

Did you know football is over 2000 years old? The first version of football was played in ancient China, where it was known as cuju. It was all about kicking a ball into a net, just like today! Football has been evolving ever since, with different countries playing their own versions of the game for centuries. The sport as we know it began to take shape in medieval Europe.

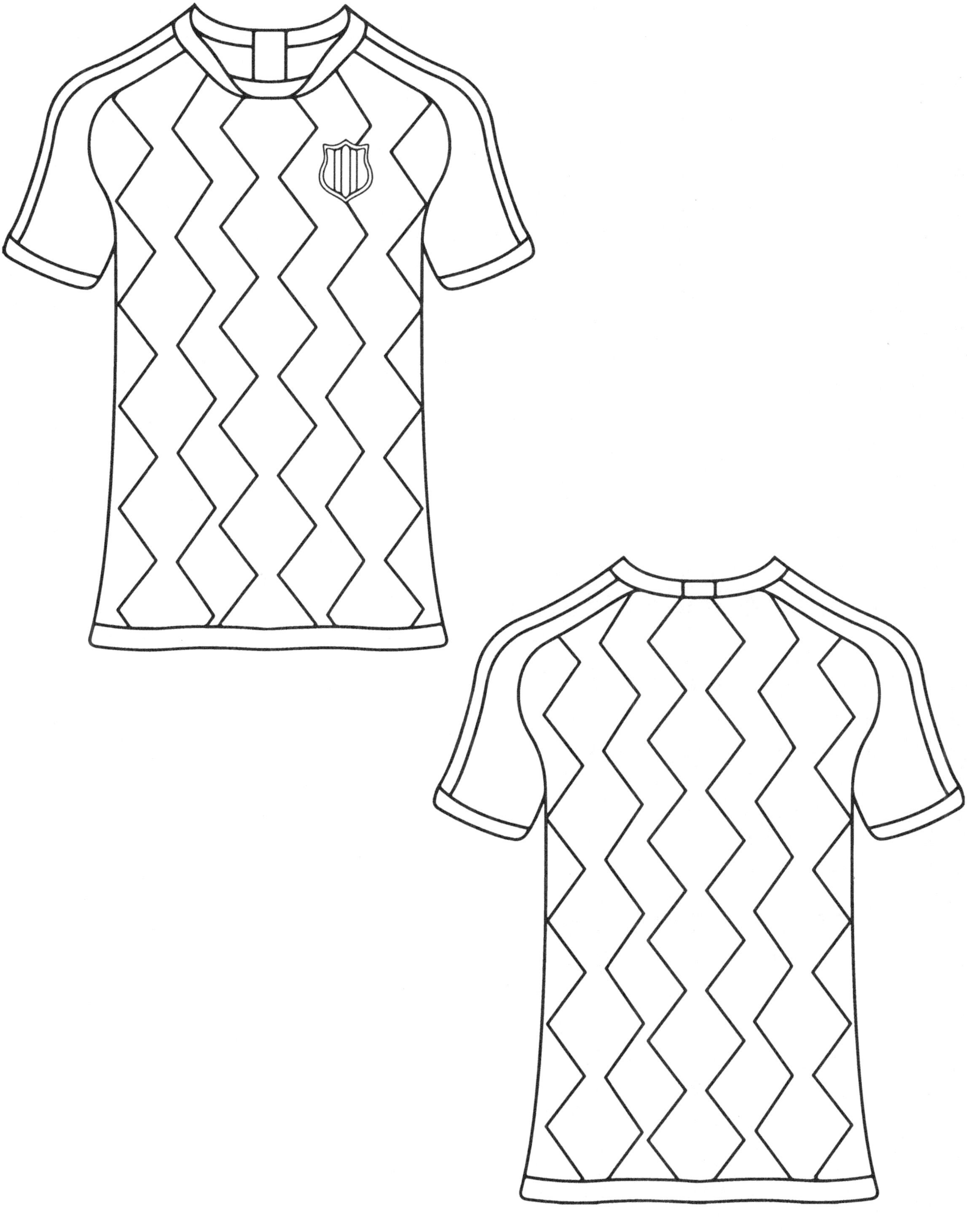

DID YOU KNOW!!

The First Ever World Cup Was in 1930! The FIFA World Cup, which is now the biggest football event in the world, started in 1930 in Uruguay. The tournament had only 13 teams, and Uruguay won the very first title by beating Argentina 4-2 in the final. Since then, the World Cup has grown into a global phenomenon!

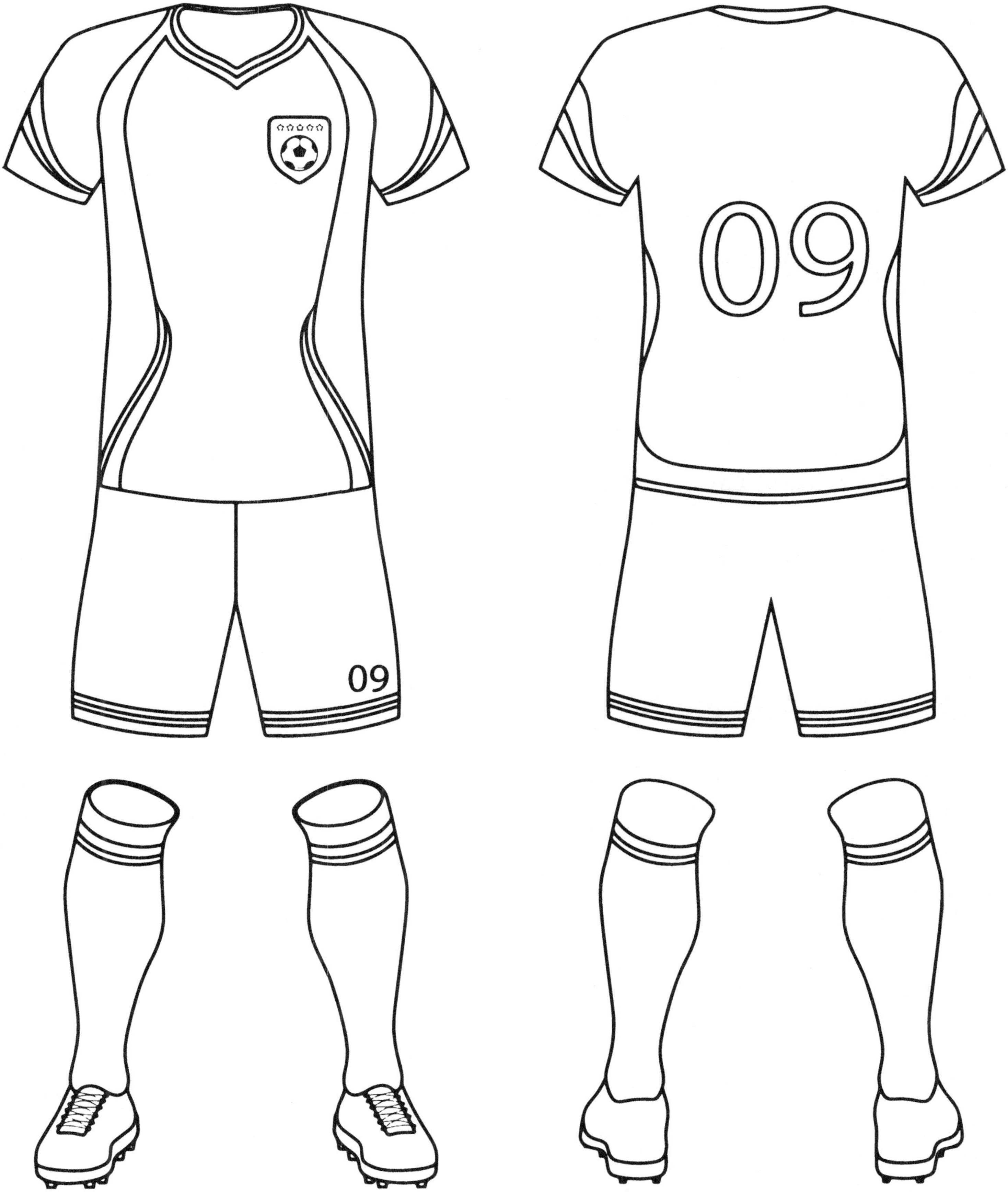
09
09

DID YOU KNOW!!

The 2022 World Cup was the first one ever held in the winter? Usually, the World Cup is played in the summer, but because of Qatar's super hot climate, the 2022 tournament was moved to November and December. Argentina won that World Cup, with Lionel Messi finally lifting the trophy!

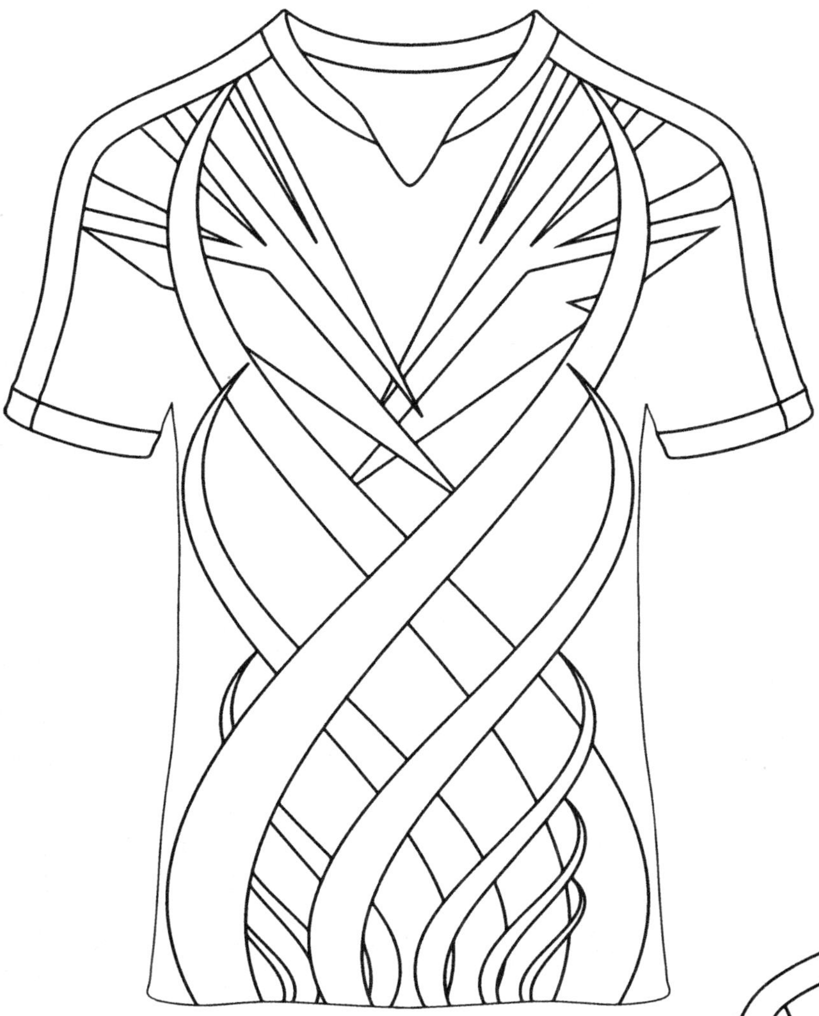

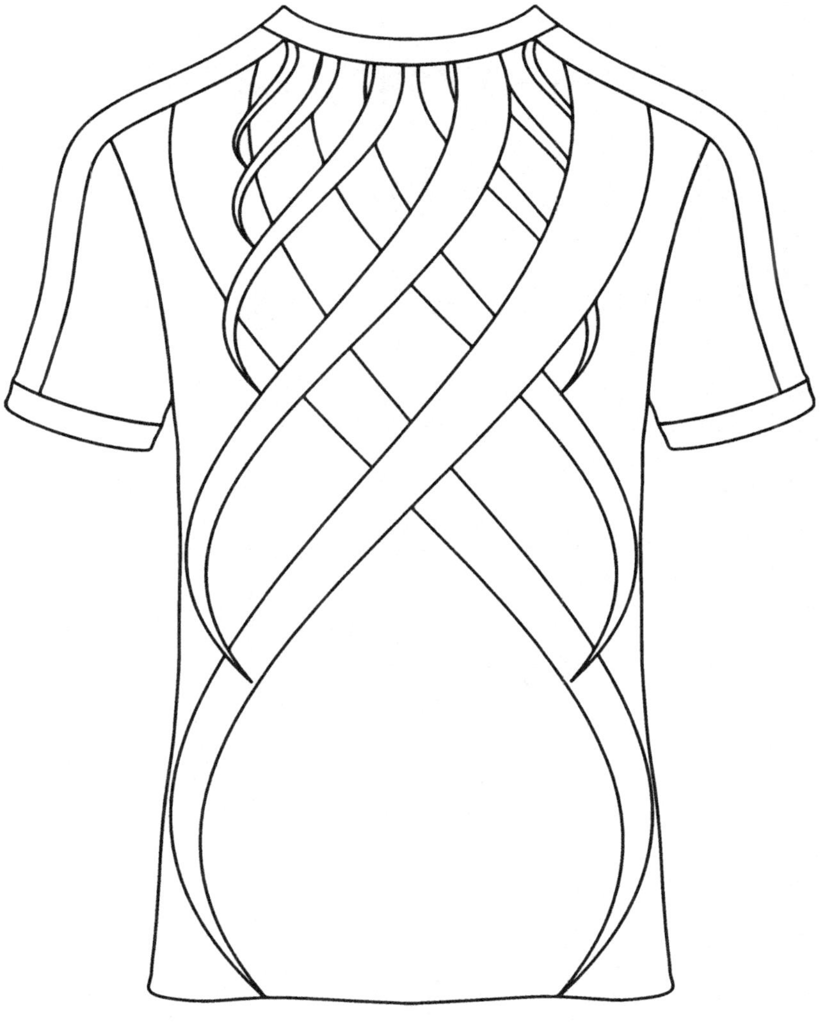

DID YOU KNOW!!

The Birth of the FA Cup in 1871! Football Association Challenge Cup (FA Cup for short), the oldest football competition in the world, began in England in 1871. It was a knockout tournament, and the first final was played in 1872 between Wanderers and Royal Engineers. Wanderers won 1-0, marking the beginning of a long tradition in English football.

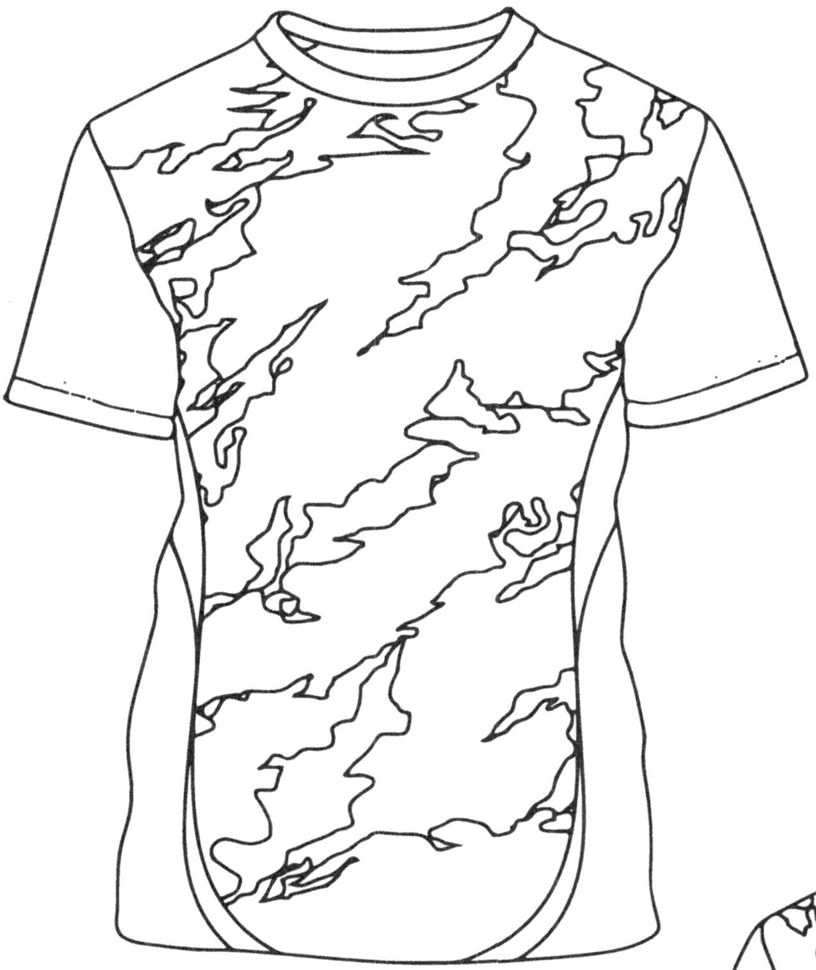

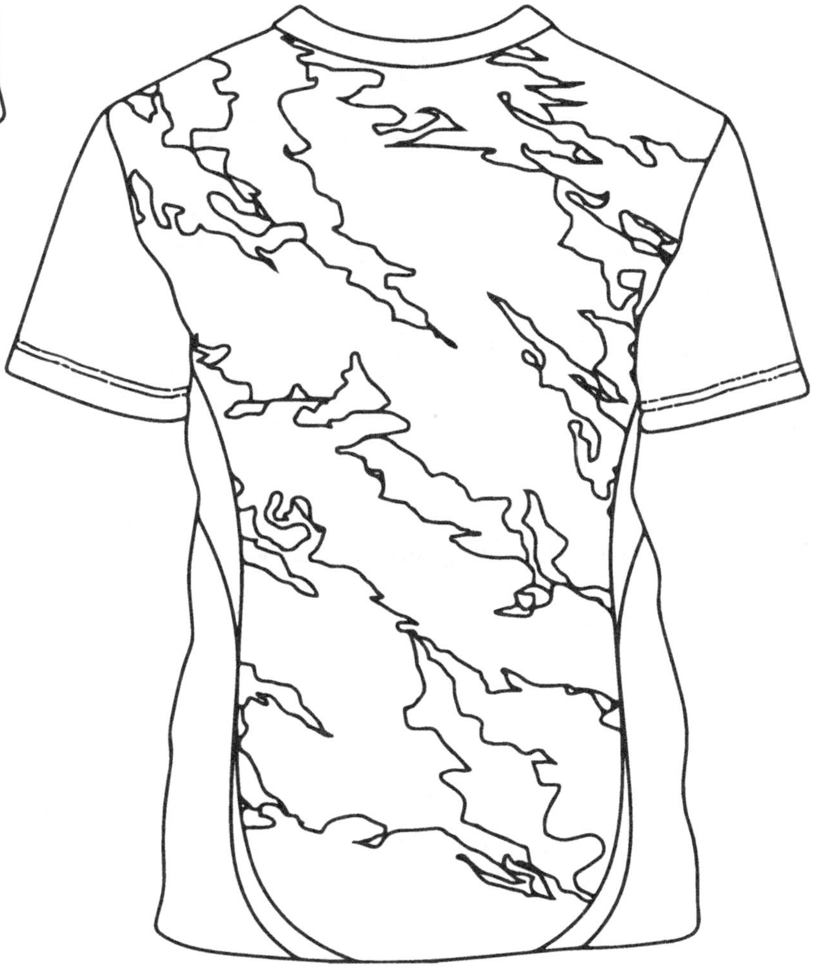

DID YOU KNOW!!

Sheffield FC: The Oldest Football Club! Founded in 1857, Sheffield Football Club in England is recognized as the oldest football club in the world. It was the first club to play by its own set of rules, which eventually influenced the development of the modern game.

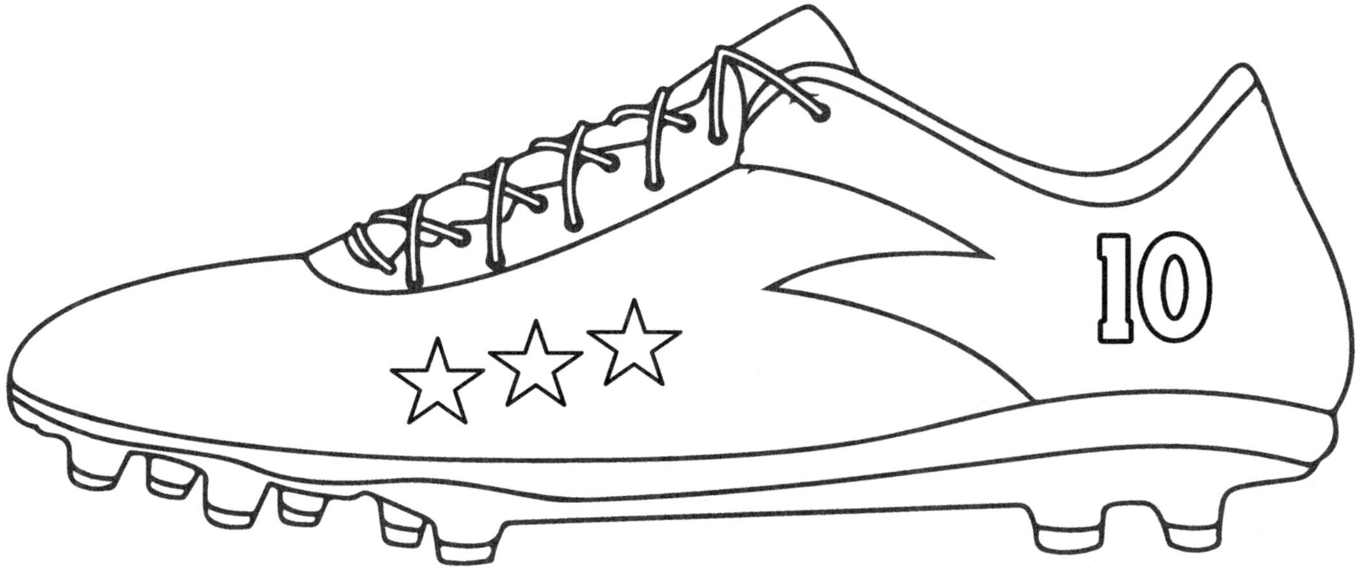
10

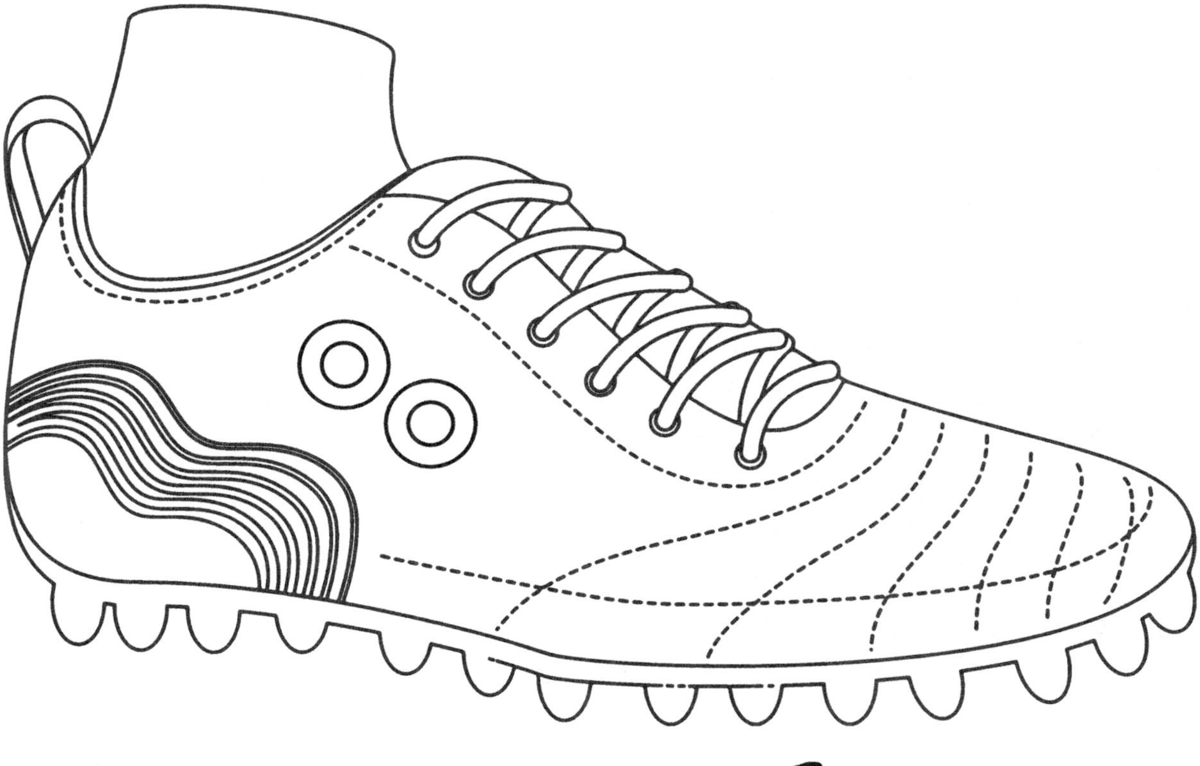

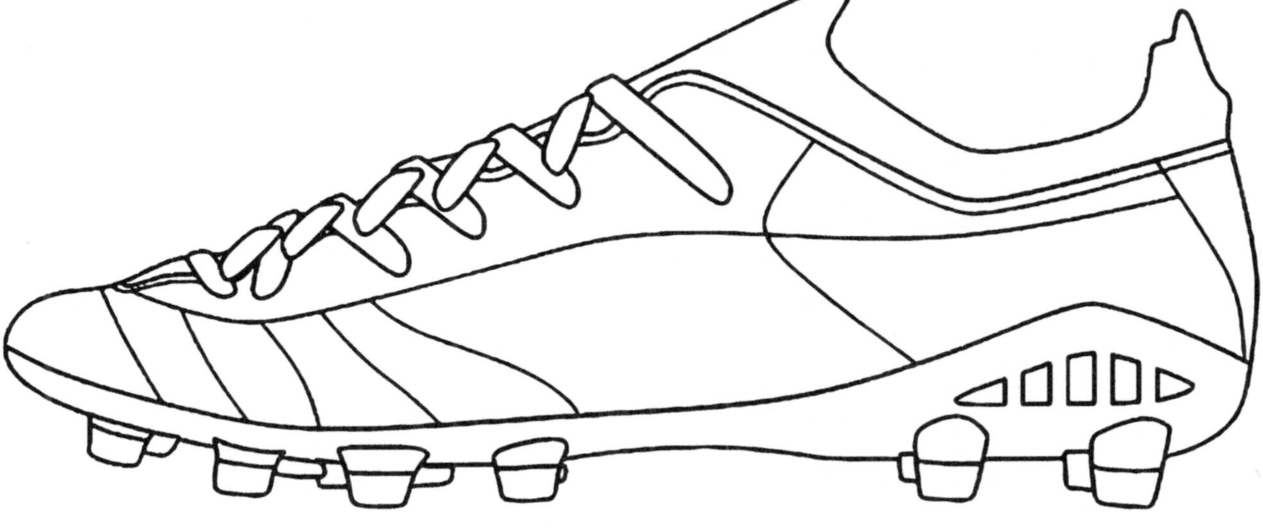

DID YOU KNOW!!

The First Red Card in a World Cup! The first-ever red card in World Cup history was shown during the 1974 tournament in West Germany. Chilean player Carlos Caszely received the red card in a match against West Germany for a foul. Since then, red cards have become a key part of maintaining fair play in football.

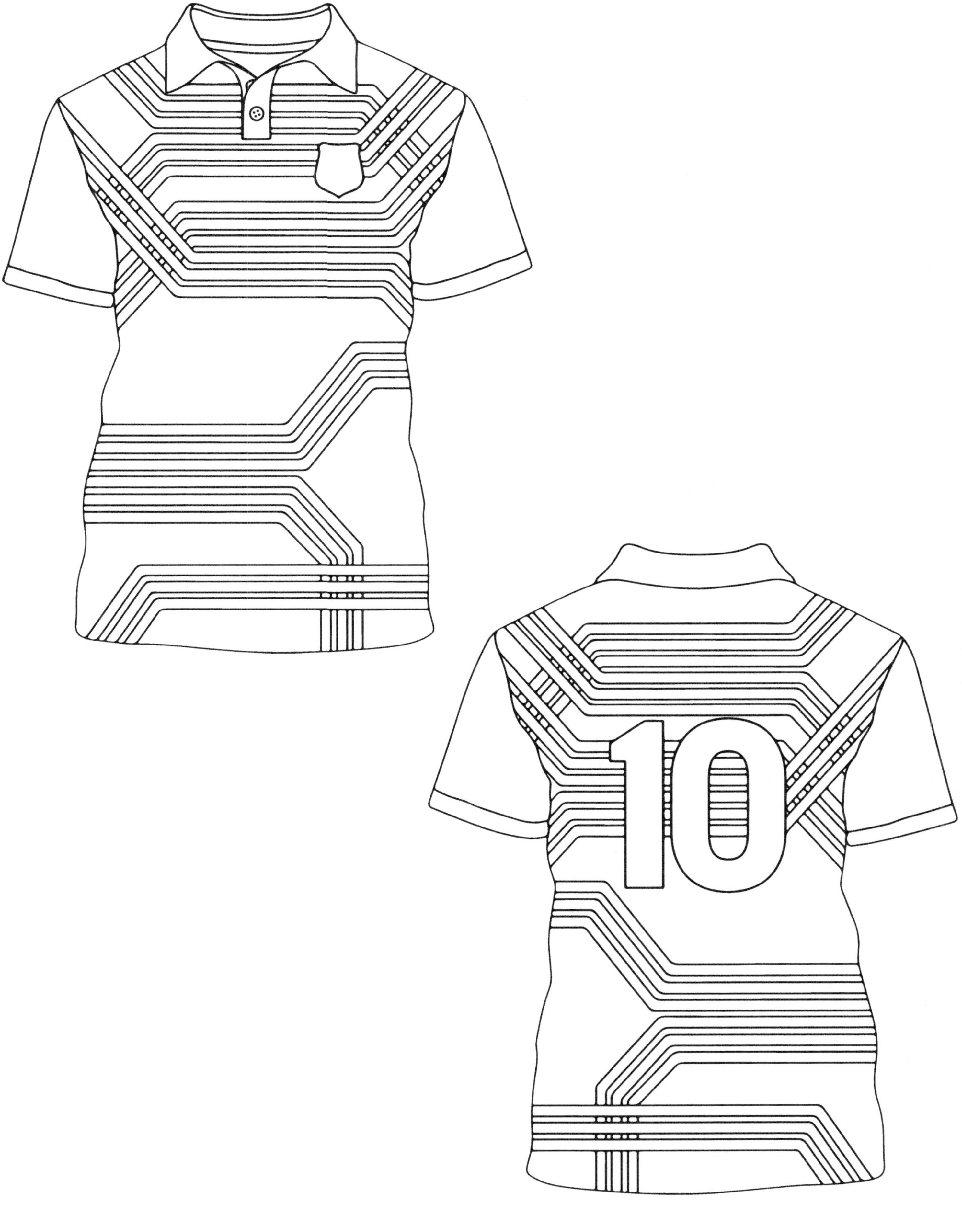
10

DID YOU KNOW!!

The First Women's World Cup Was in 1991! The inaugural FIFA Women's World Cup was held in China in 1991. The United States won the first tournament, defeating Norway 2-1 in the final. Since then, women's football has grown tremendously, with the World Cup becoming a major global event.

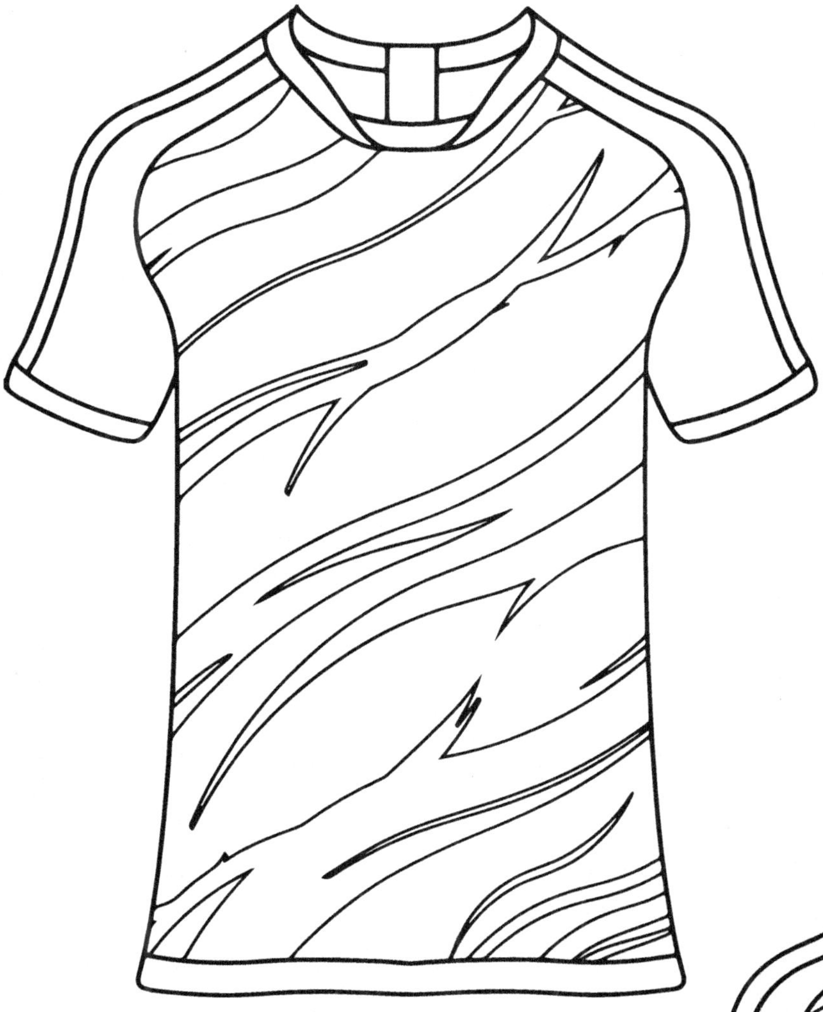

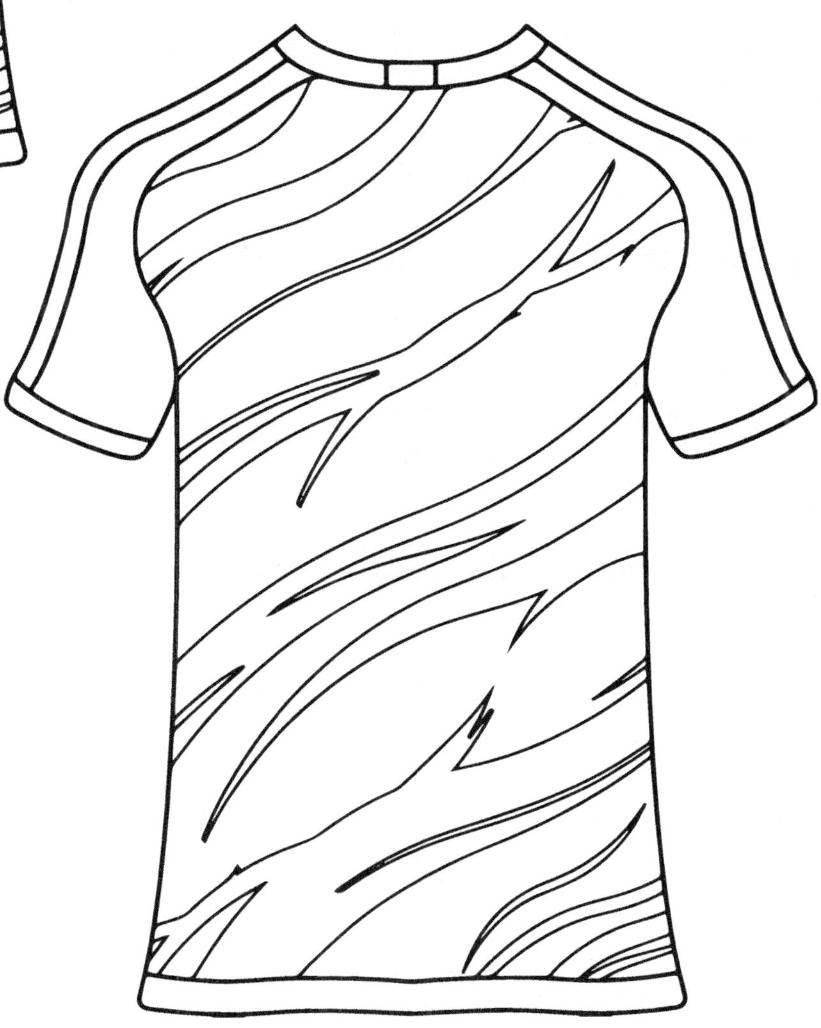

DID YOU KNOW!!

The Women's World Cup is getting bigger and bigger! The 2023 Women's World Cup in Australia and New Zealand was the largest yet, with 32 teams competing. Spain won the tournament, their first Women's World Cup victory! The event is inspiring more girls worldwide to play football.

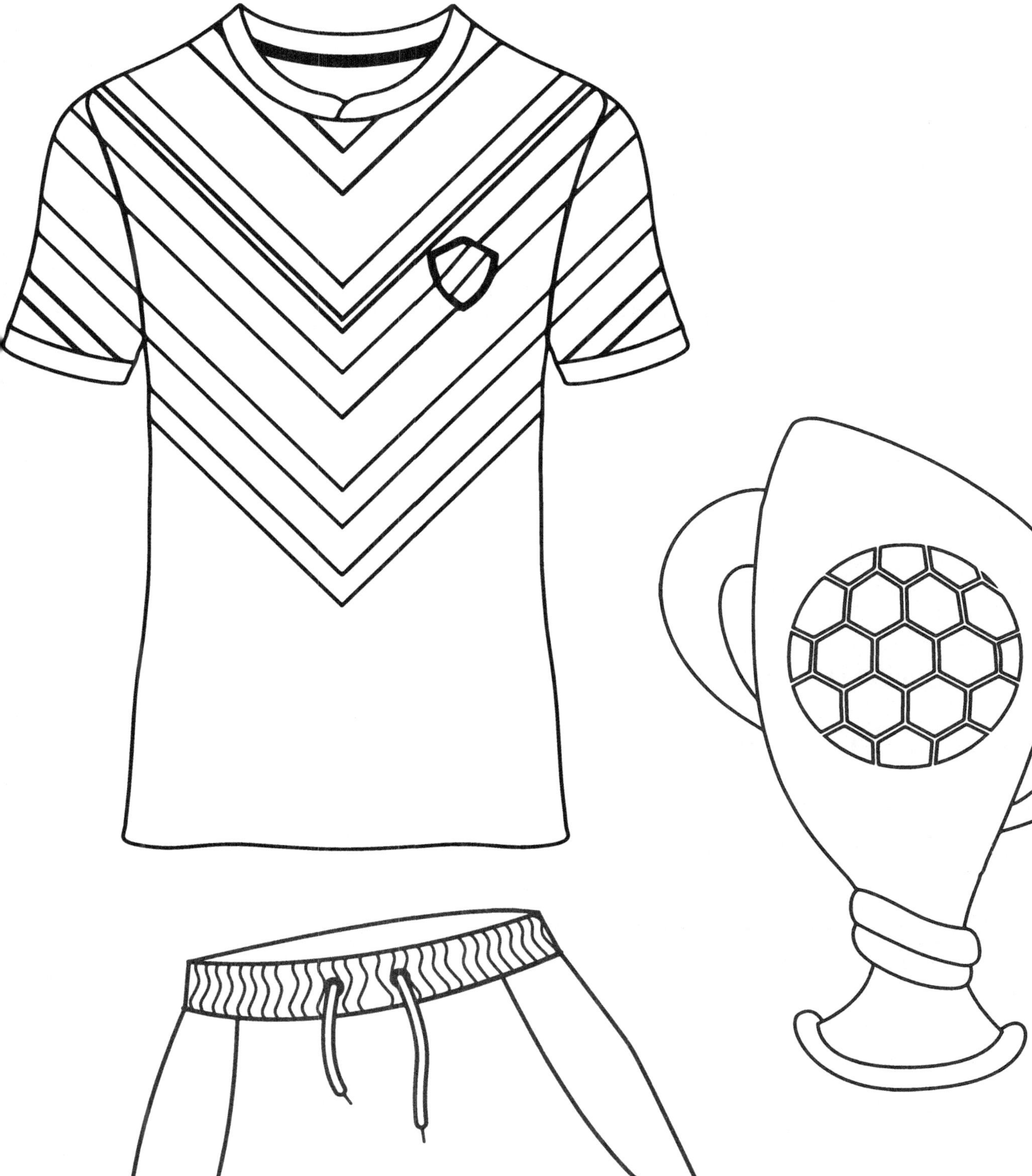

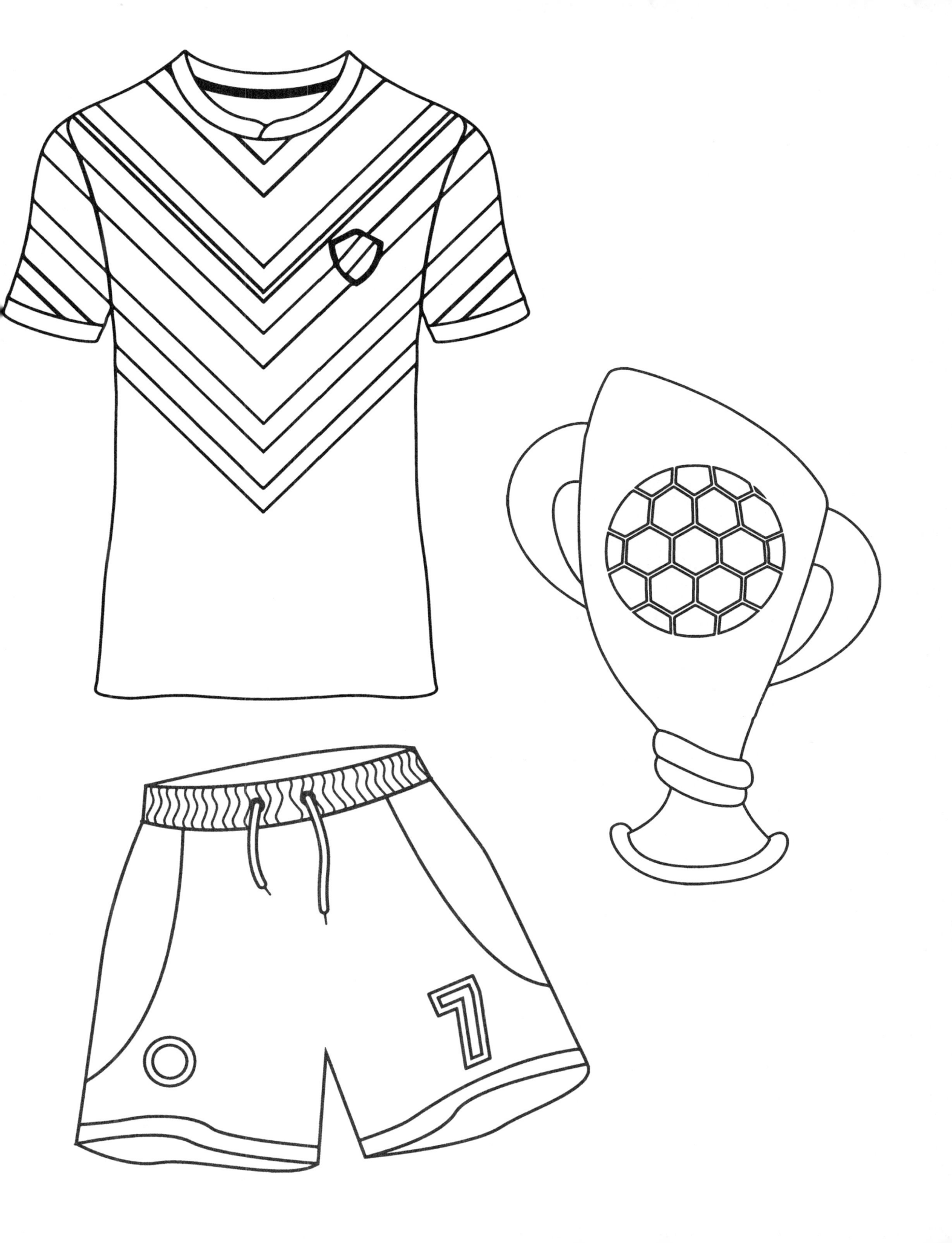

DID YOU KNOW!!

Cristiano Ronaldo has played for clubs in four different countries! Ronaldo started his career in Portugal, then moved to England to play for Manchester United, went on to play for Real Madrid in Spain, Juventus in Italy, and now he's playing in Saudi Arabia! He's one of the few players to shine in so many leagues.

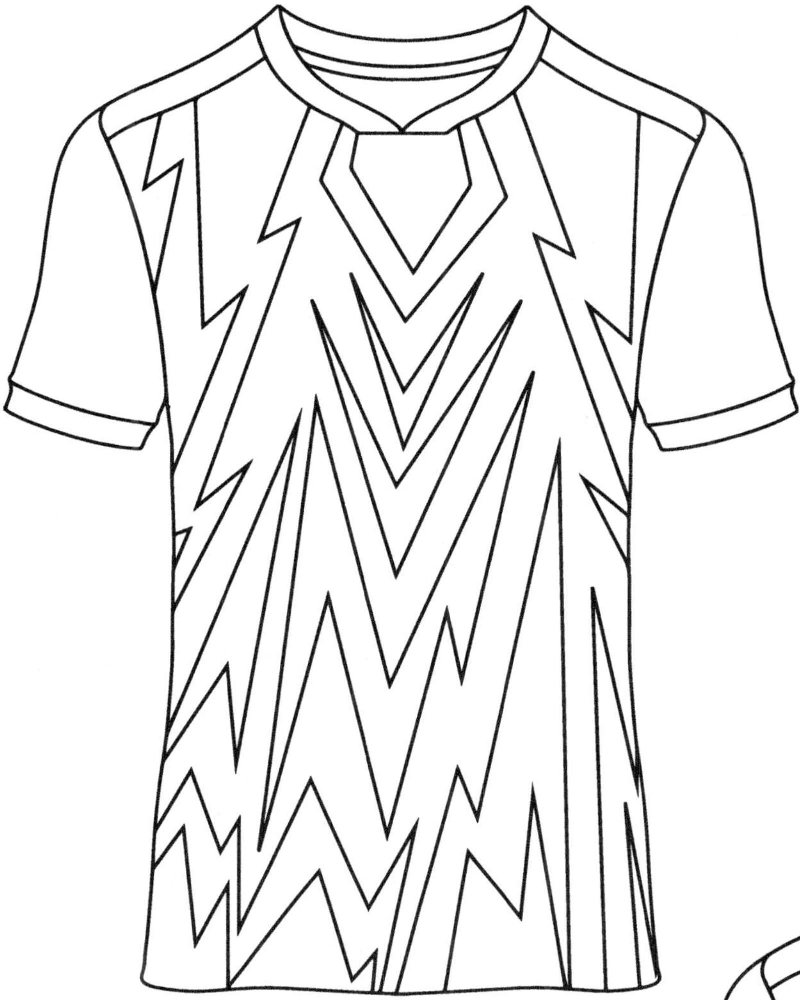

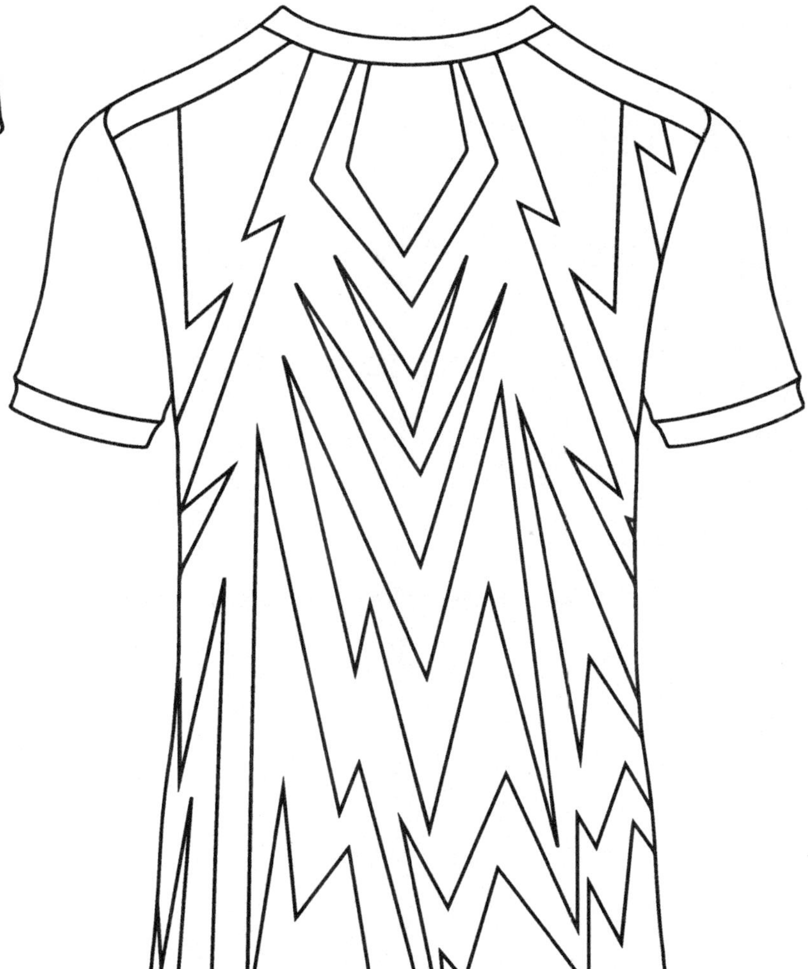

DID YOU KNOW!!

VAR is Changing the Game! VAR, which stands for Video Assistant Referee, was introduced at the 2018 FIFA World Cup in Russia to help referees make better decisions using video replays. While it's made football fairer by correcting mistakes, it's also sparked plenty of debate among fans and players. Whether you love it or hate it, VAR is now a big part of football!

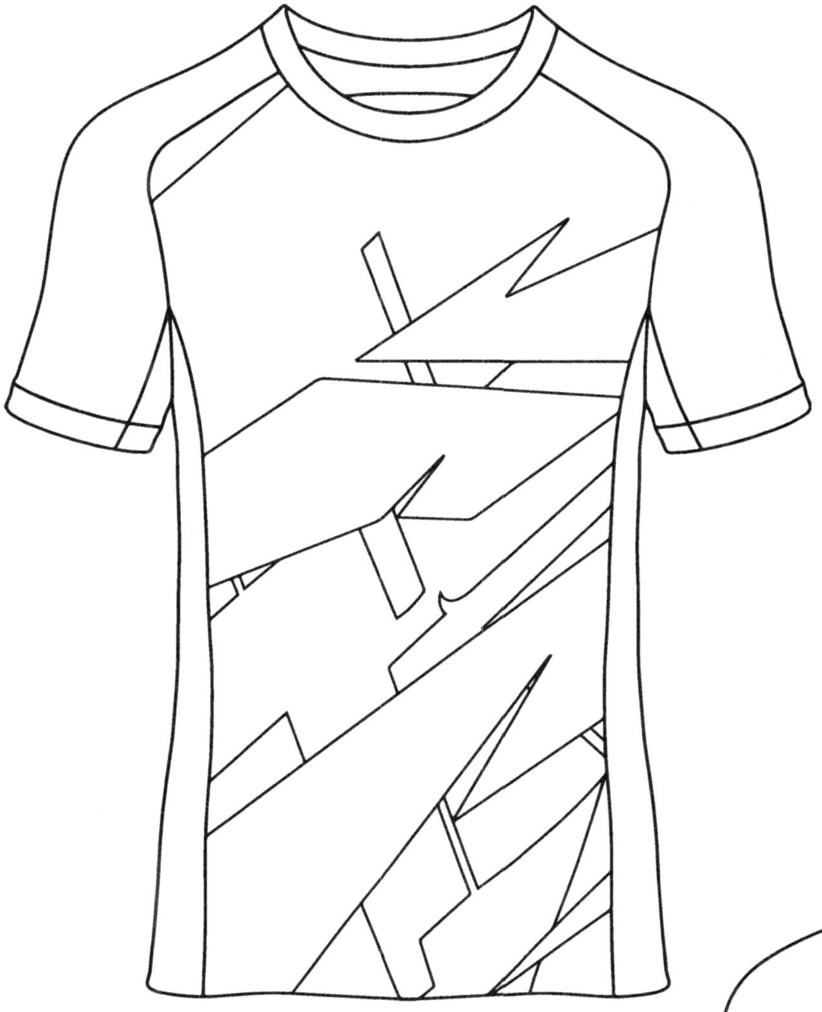

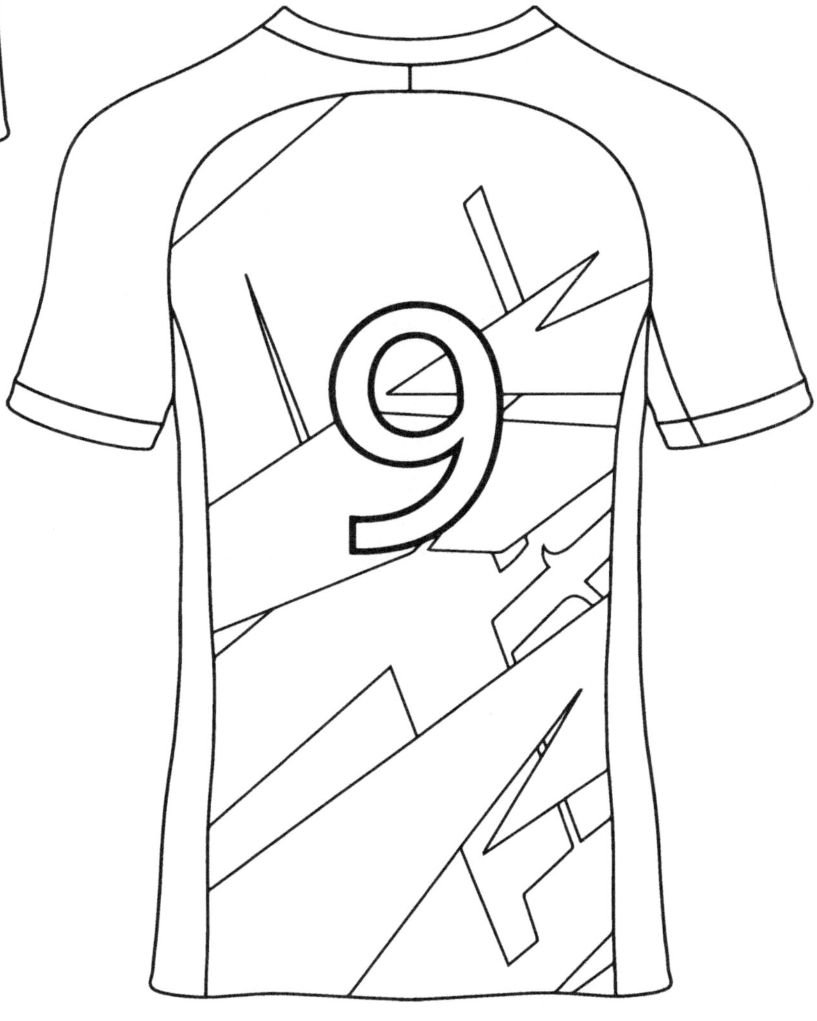
9

DID YOU KNOW!!

The Invention of the Offside Rule! The offside rule, one of the most important rules in football, was first introduced in 1863 by the newly formed Football Association in England. The rule has evolved over time to make the game more exciting and fair, preventing players from just waiting near the opponent's goal to score.

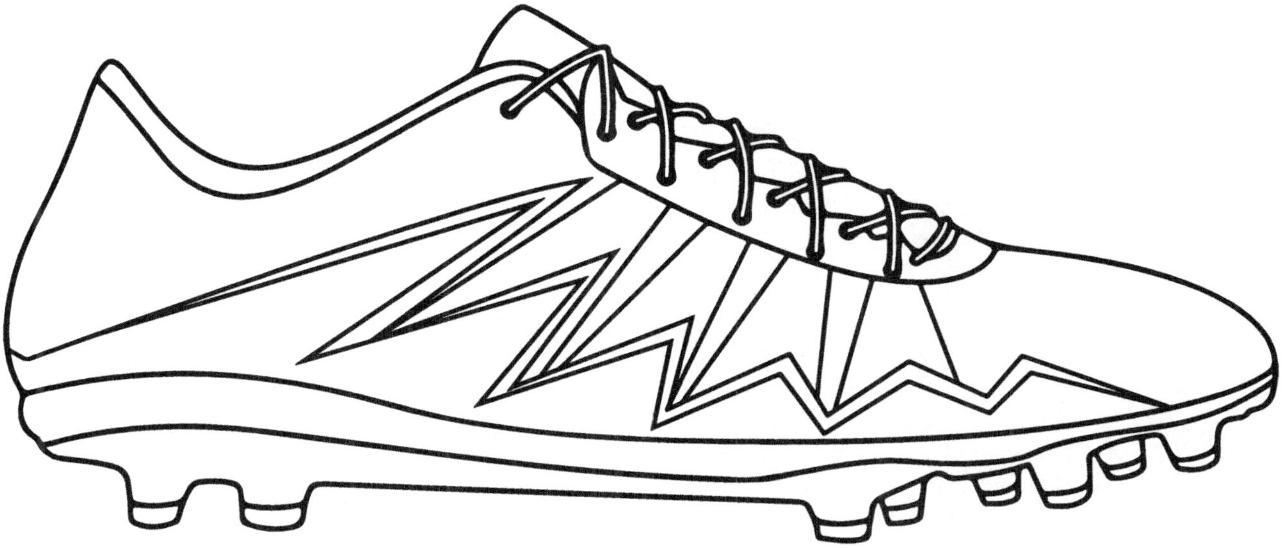

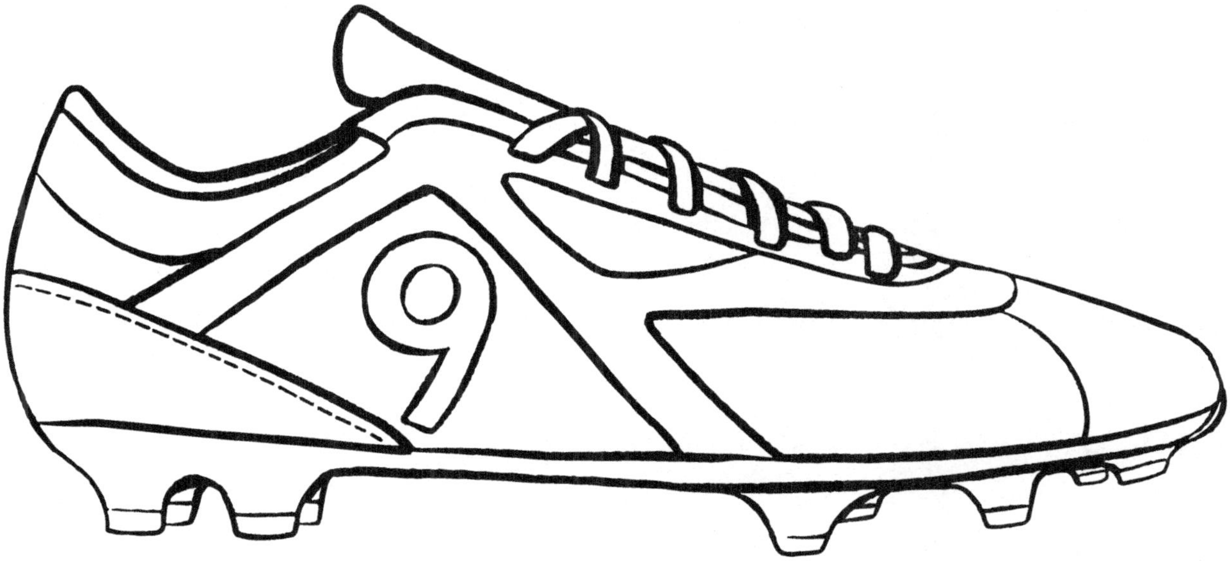
9

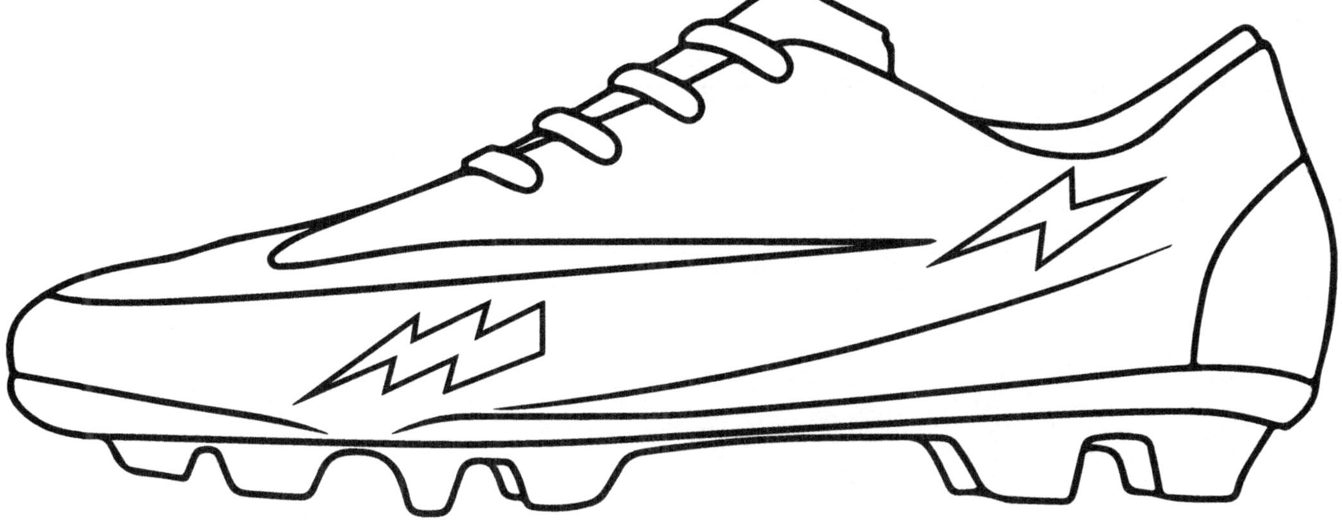

DID YOU KNOW!!

The Founding of FIFA in 1904! FIFA, the international governing body of football, was founded in Paris, France, on May 21, 1904. It was created to oversee international football matches between countries. Today, FIFA organizes the World Cup, the biggest football tournament in the world.

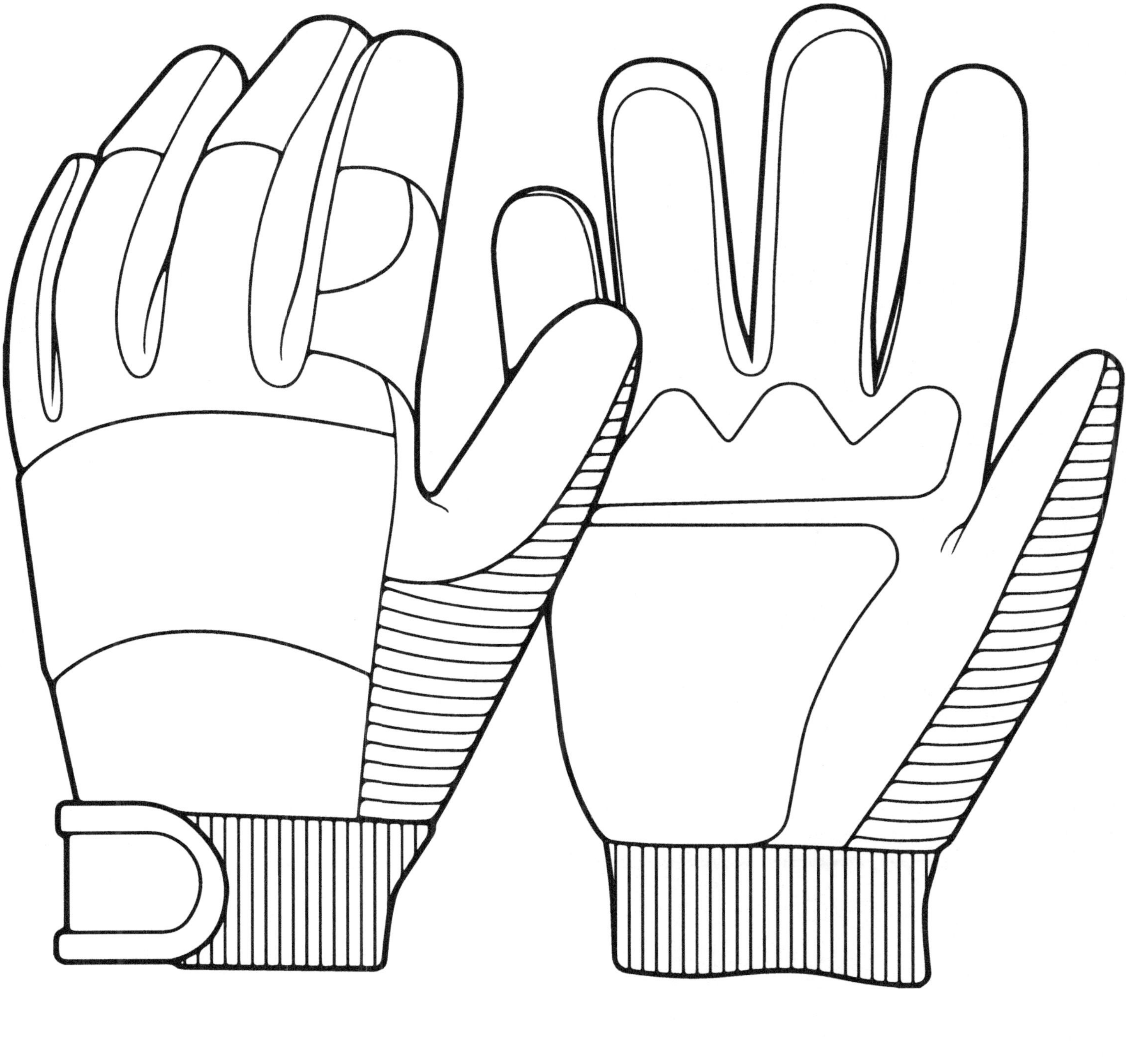

DID YOU KNOW!!

The First Ever Penalty Kick! The penalty kick was introduced in 1891 to punish serious fouls in football. The first-ever penalty in a professional match was awarded to Wolverhampton Wanderers in a game against Accrington. It's now a crucial part of the game, often deciding the outcome of matches.

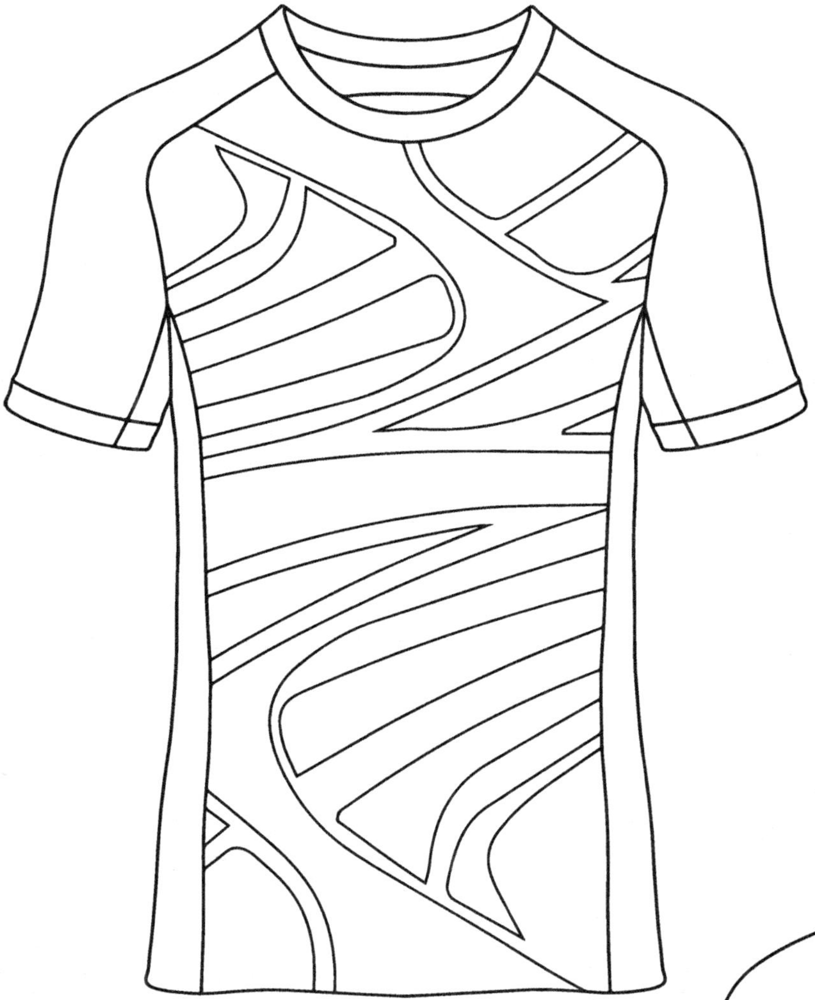

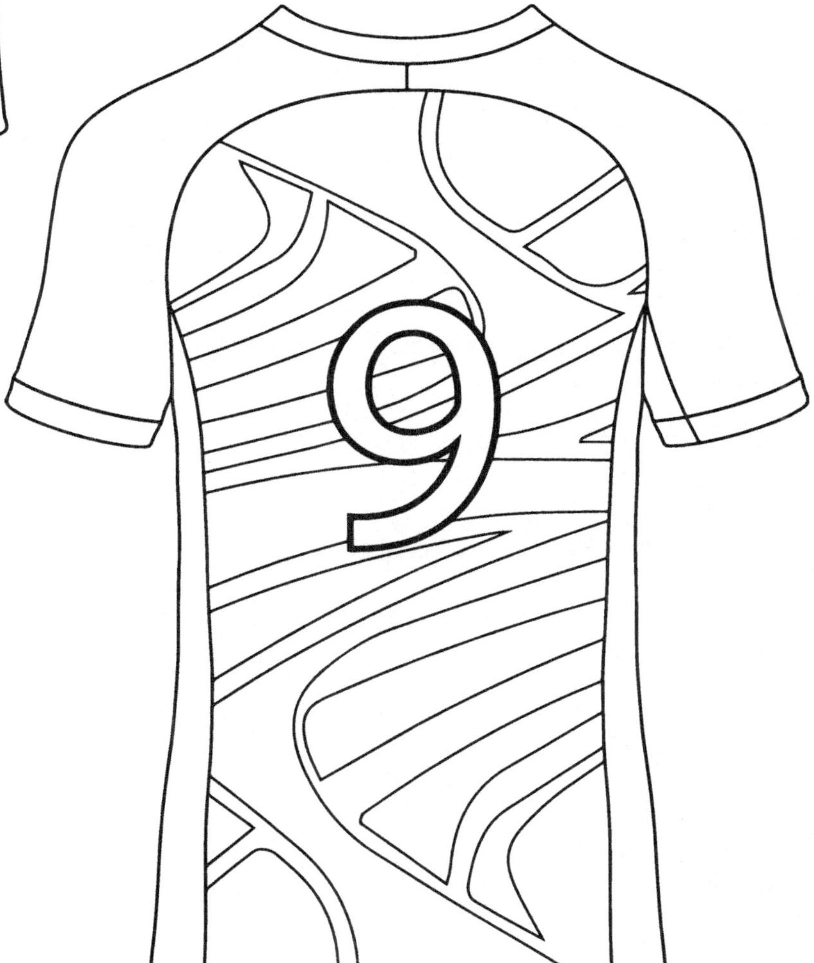
9

DID YOU KNOW!!

The Birth of the UEFA Champions League! The UEFA Champions League, Europe's premier club competition, started in 1955. Originally called the European Cup, it featured the top teams from across Europe. Real Madrid won the first five titles, establishing themselves as a football powerhouse.

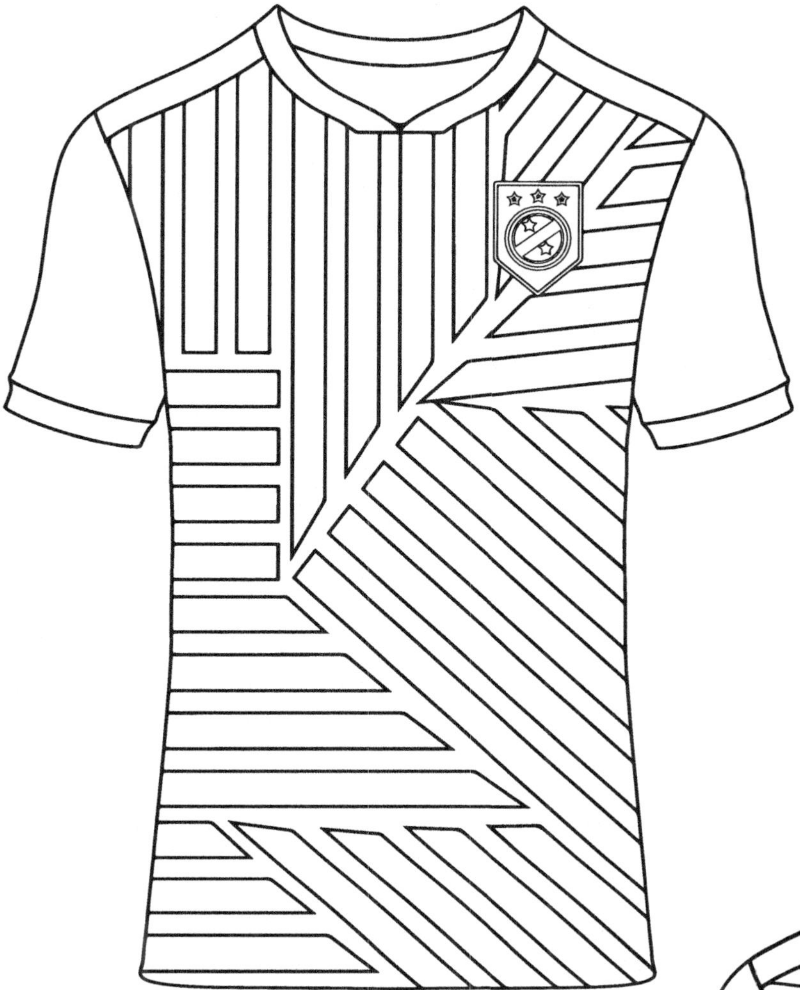
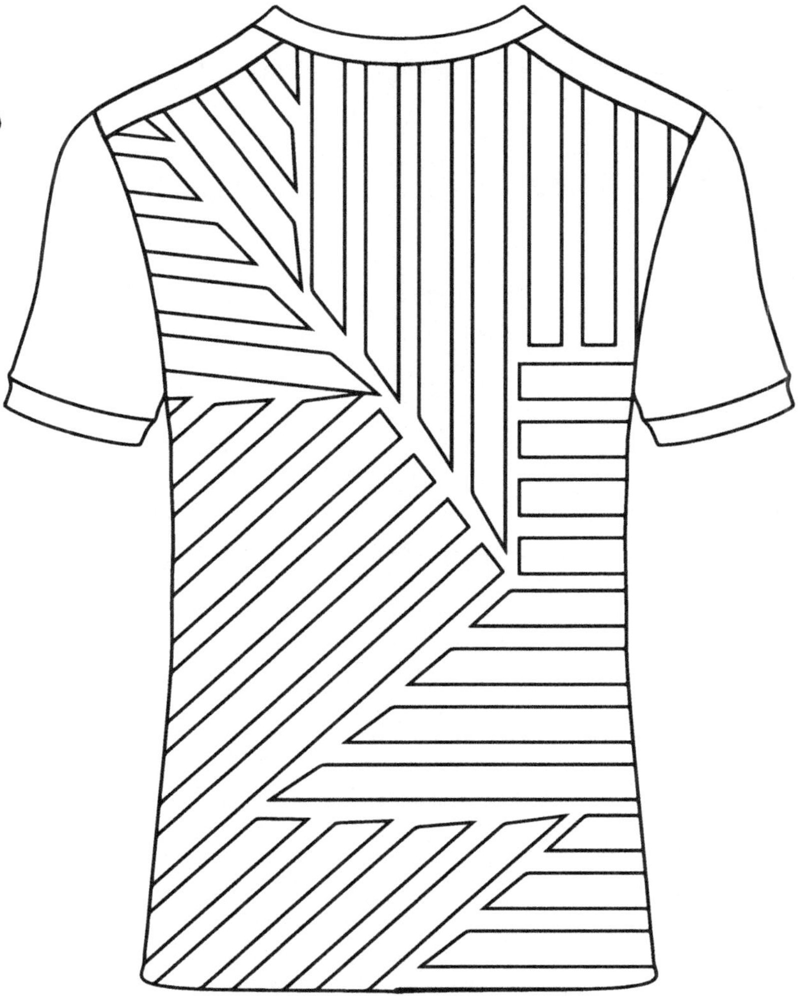

DID YOU KNOW!!

The First Televised Football Match! The first football match to be broadcast on television was an exhibition game between Arsenal and Arsenal Reserves in 1937. The match was shown on the BBC, and it marked the beginning of football's long relationship with television, bringing the game into homes around the world.

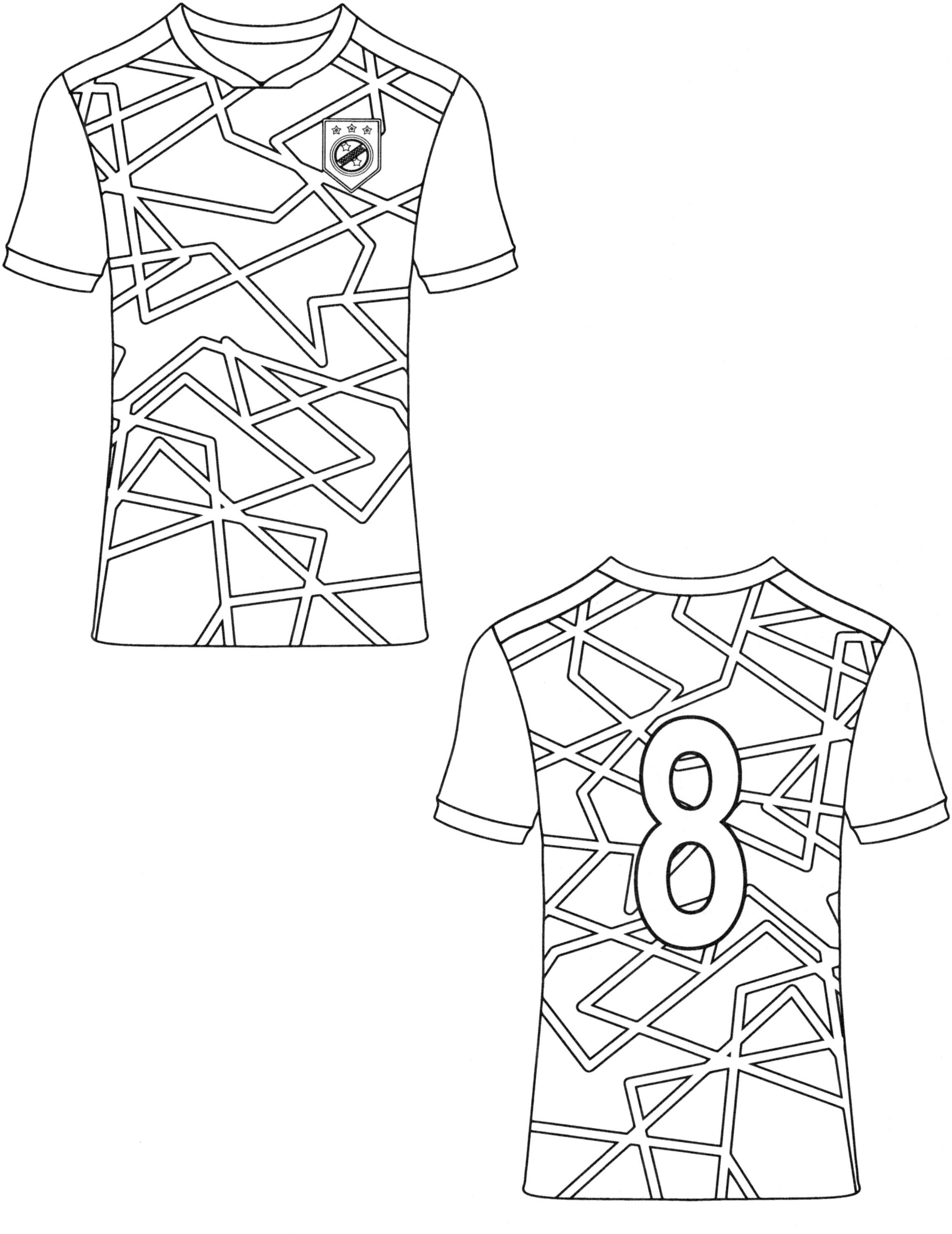
8

DID YOU KNOW!!

The First African Team to Play in the World Cup! Egypt was the first African country to participate in the FIFA World Cup in 1934. Although they were eliminated in the first round, their participation marked the beginning of Africa's involvement in the world's most famous football tournament.

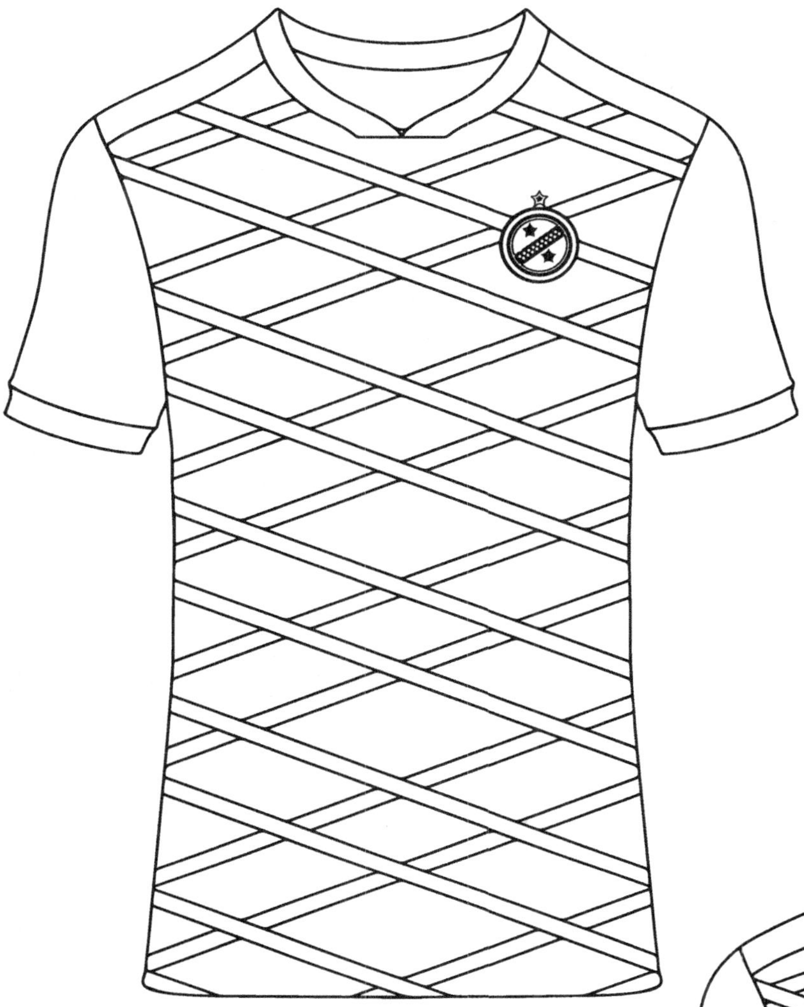
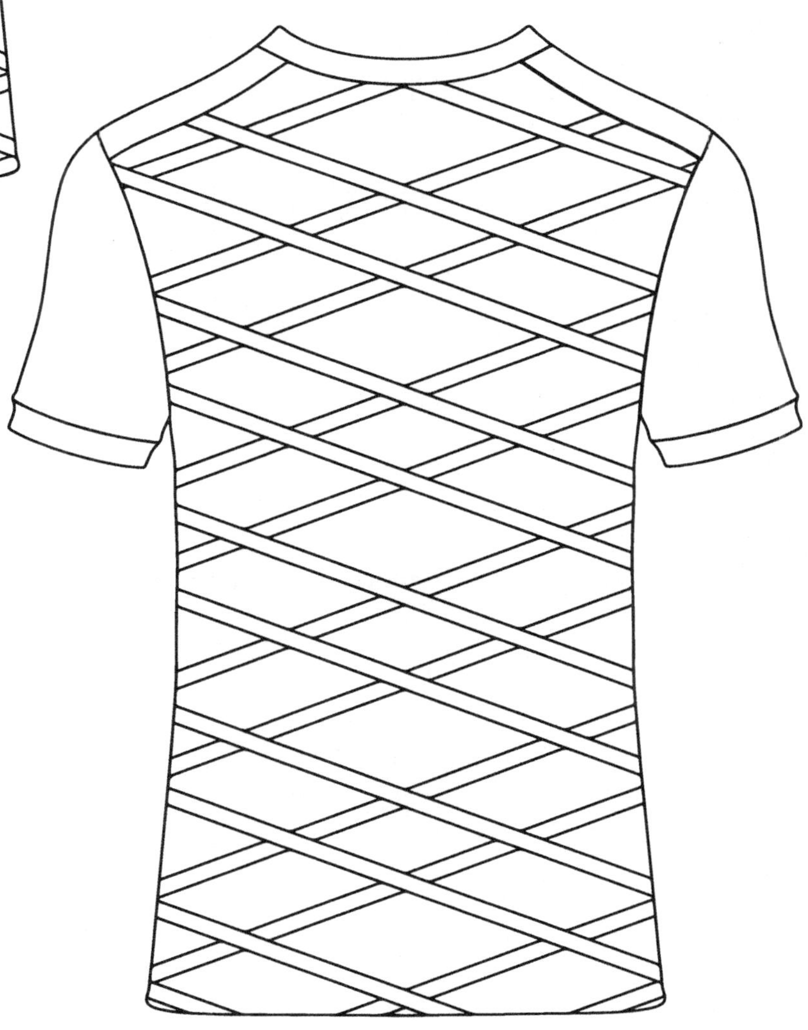

DID YOU KNOW!!

The First Women's World Cup: The first FIFA Women's World Cup was held in 1991 in China, with the USA emerging as the champions. This tournament marked the beginning of what has become a major event in women's sports.

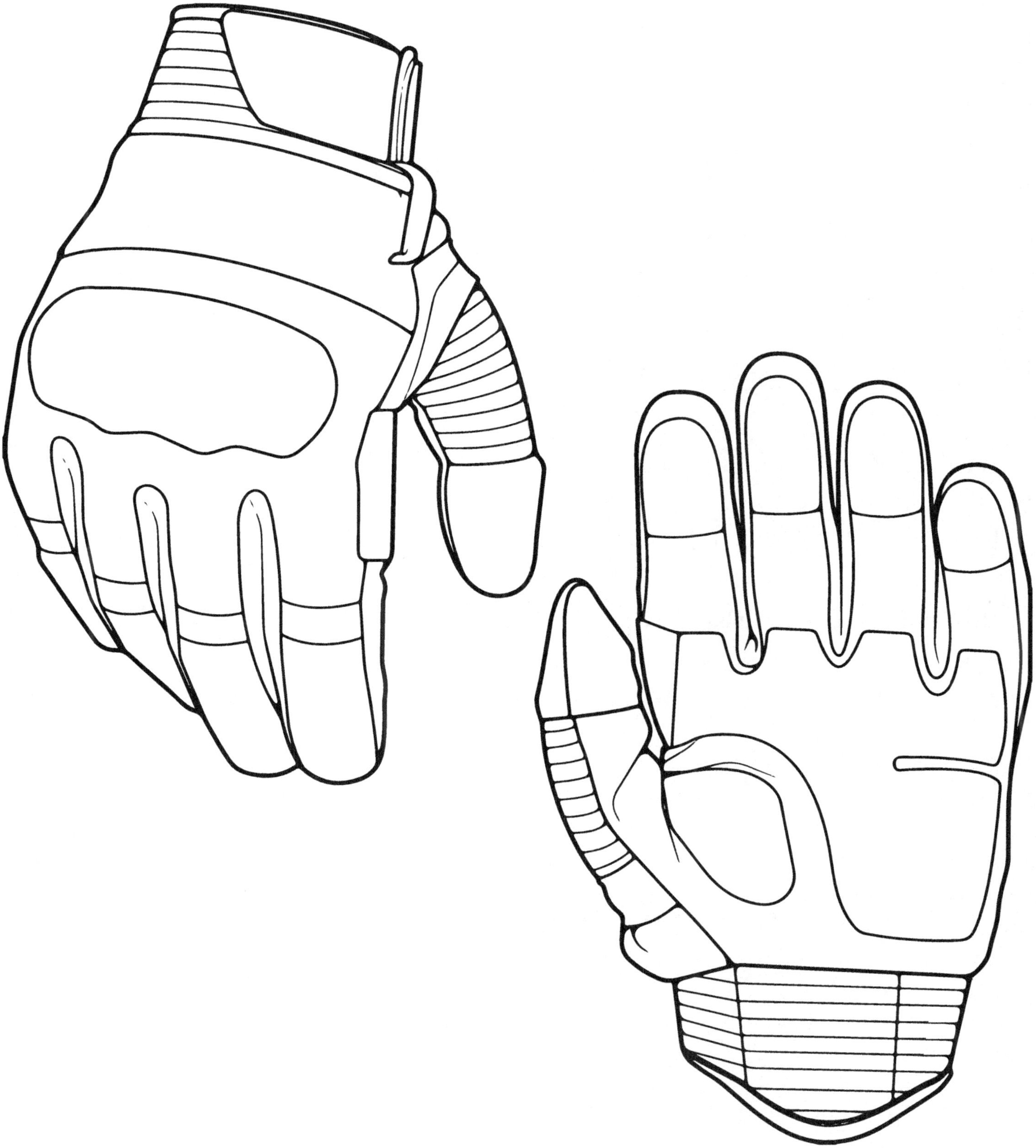

DID YOU KNOW!!

Premier League's First 100-Point Season: In 2018, Manchester City became the first team in Premier League history to reach 100 points in a single season, under the management of Pep Guardiola. This record-breaking performance showcased their dominance in English football.

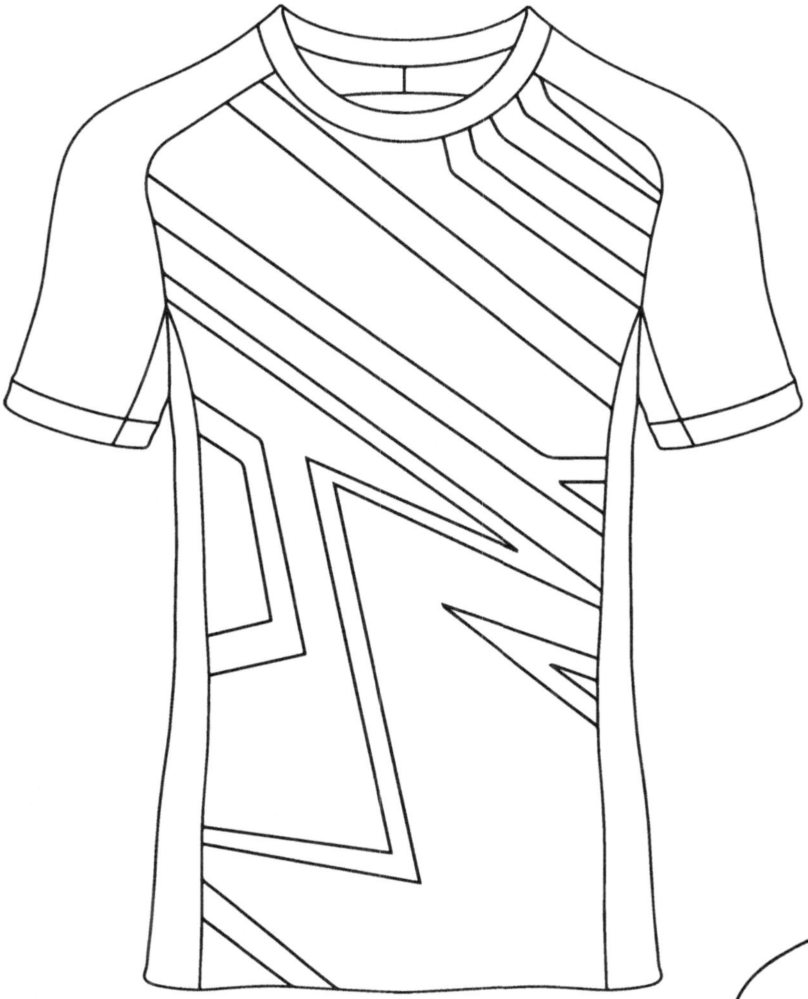

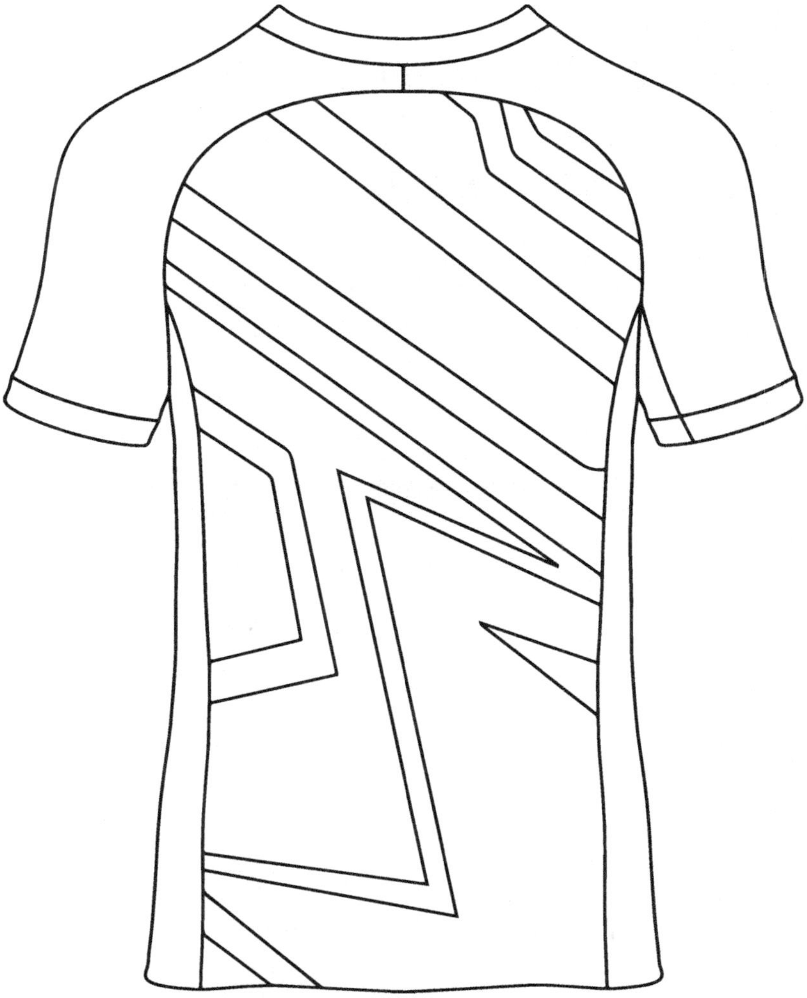

DID YOU KNOW!!

Messi's Record 8th Ballon d'Or: In 2023, Lionel Messi won his record-breaking 8th Ballon d'Or, solidifying his place as one of the greatest footballers in history. His remarkable career has been filled with numerous records and incredible performances.

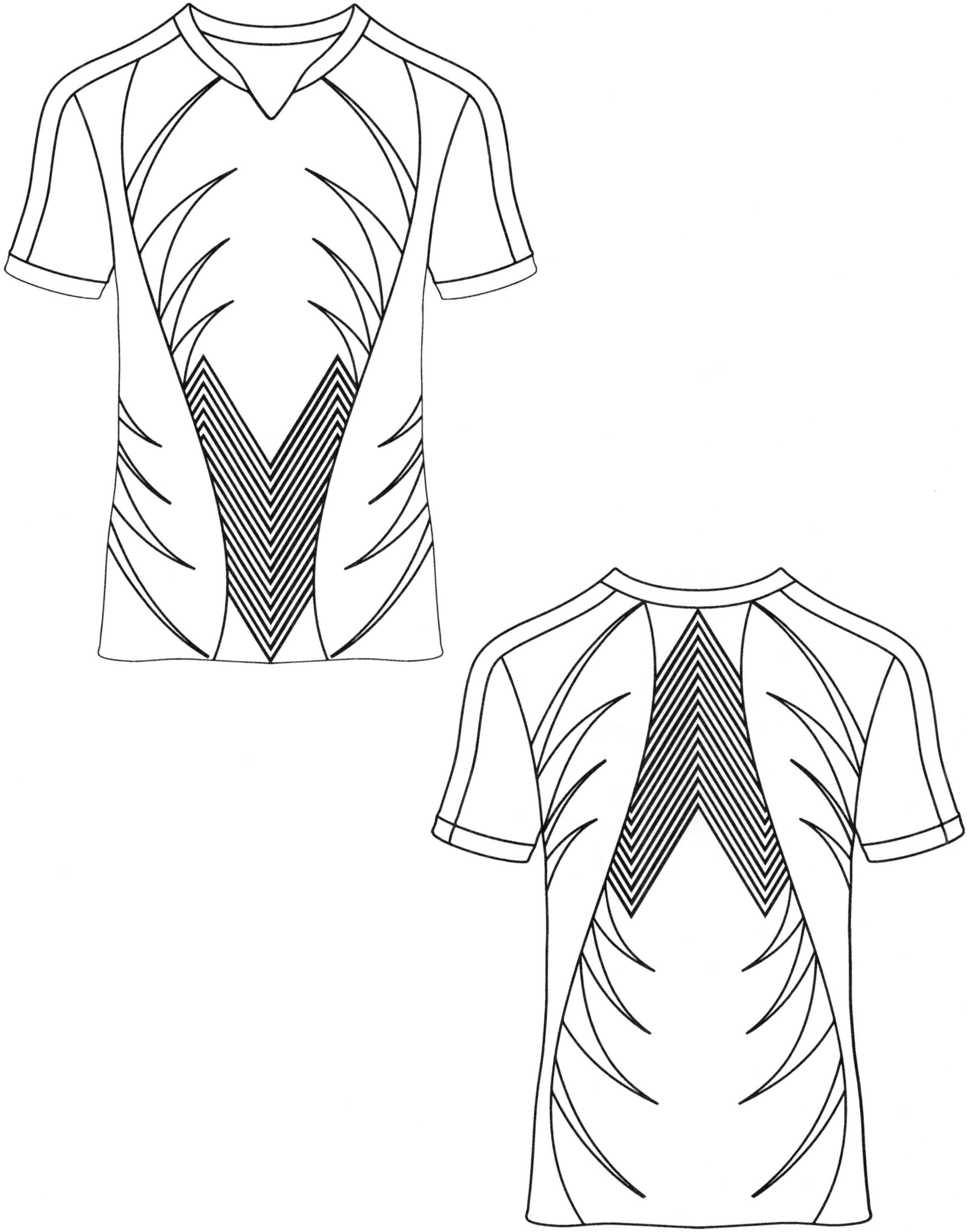

DID YOU KNOW!!

The Invincibles of Arsenal: In the 2003-2004 Premier League season, Arsenal completed an entire season unbeaten, earning the nickname "The Invincibles." Managed by Arsène Wenger, they won 26 matches and drew 12, a record that still stands today.

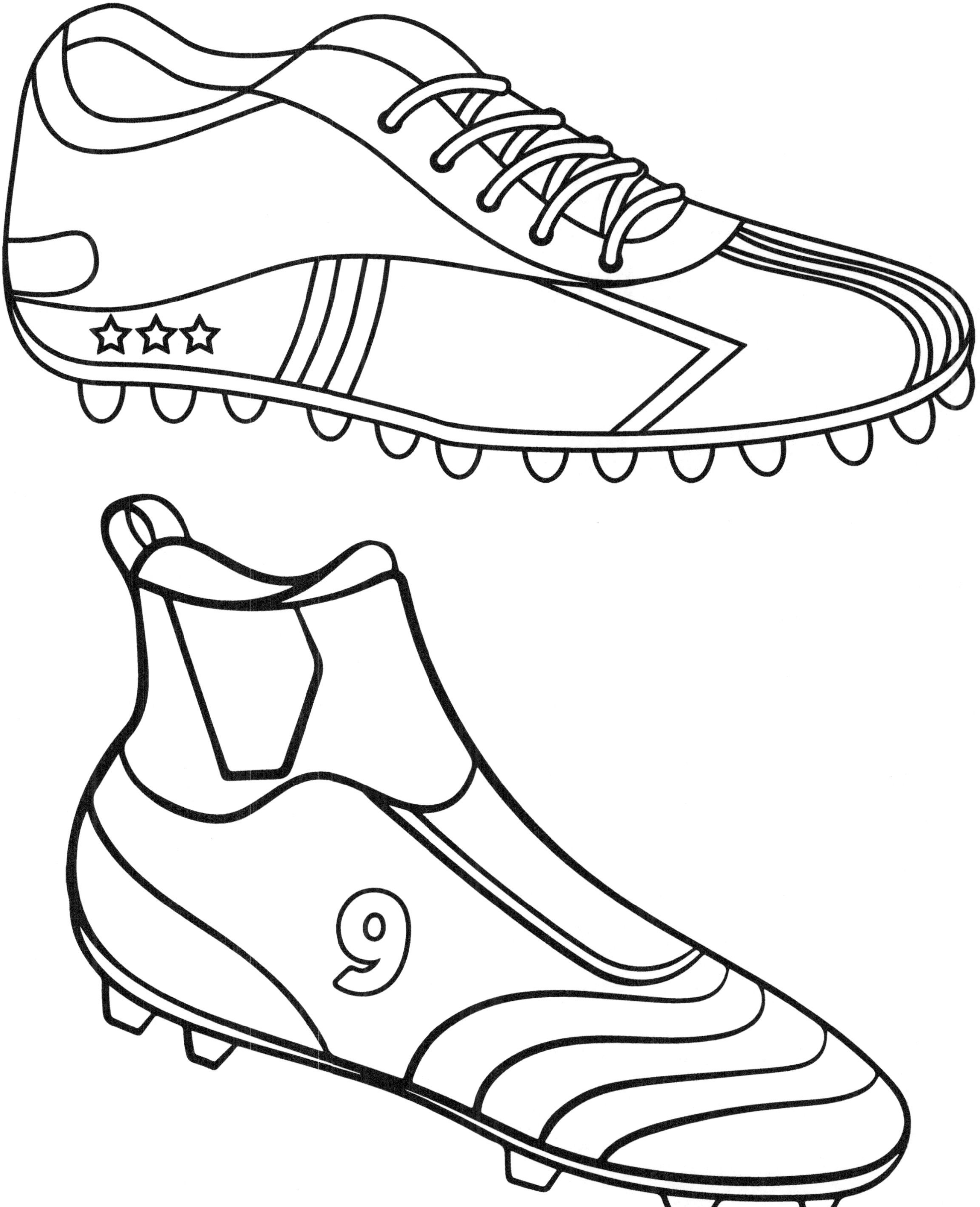
9

DID YOU KNOW!!

Women's World Cup Viewership Soars: The 2023 FIFA Women's World Cup set new viewership records, with over 2 billion people tuning in to watch the tournament. This highlights the growing popularity and significance of women's football worldwide.

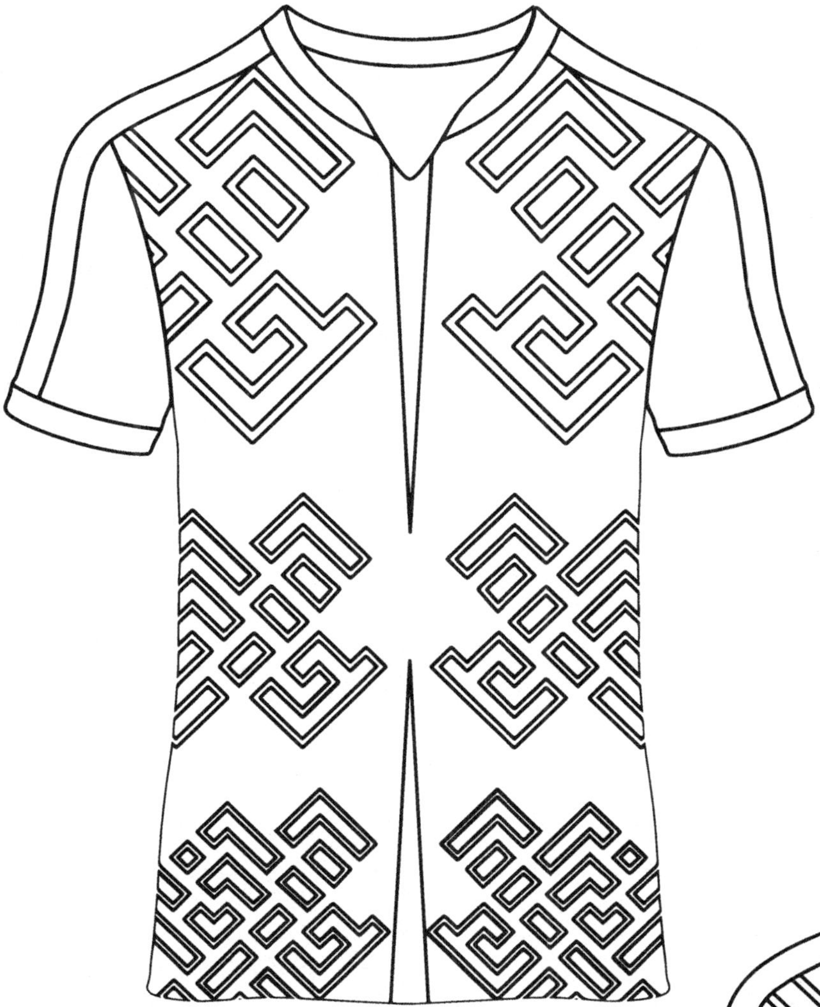
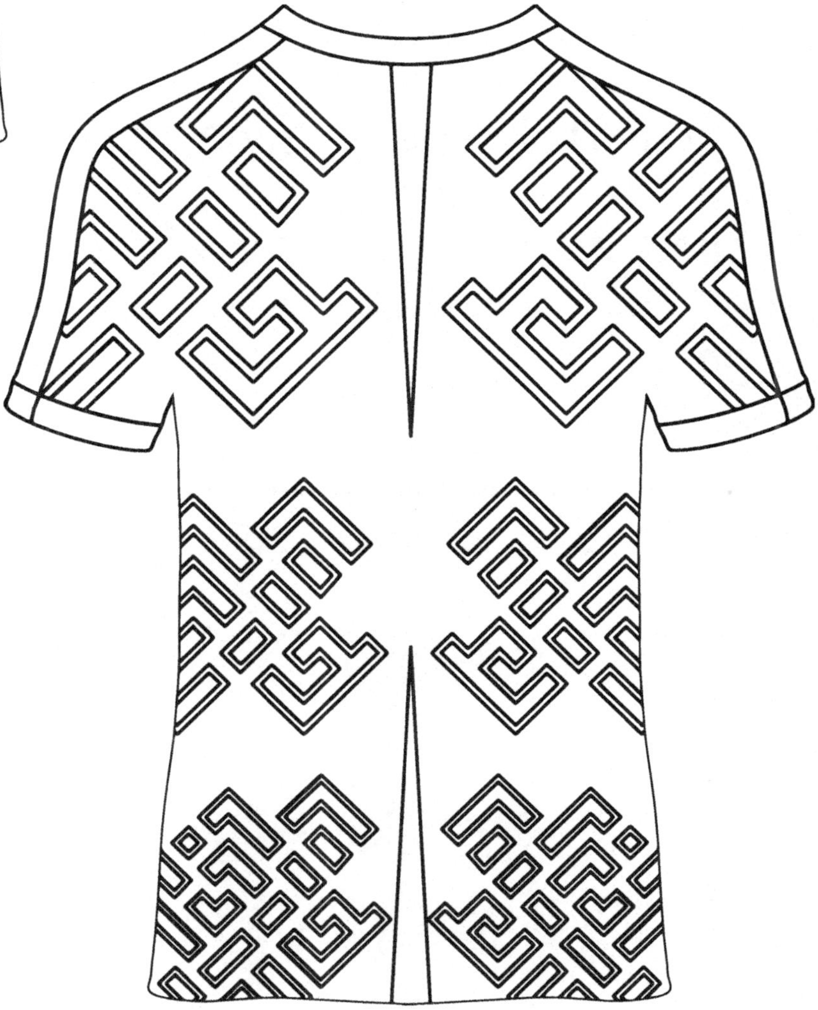

DID YOU KNOW!!

First Use of Goal-Line Technology: Goal-line technology was first used in the 2014 FIFA World Cup in Brazil. The system ensures that referees can accurately determine whether the ball has fully crossed the goal line, eliminating controversial "ghost goals"

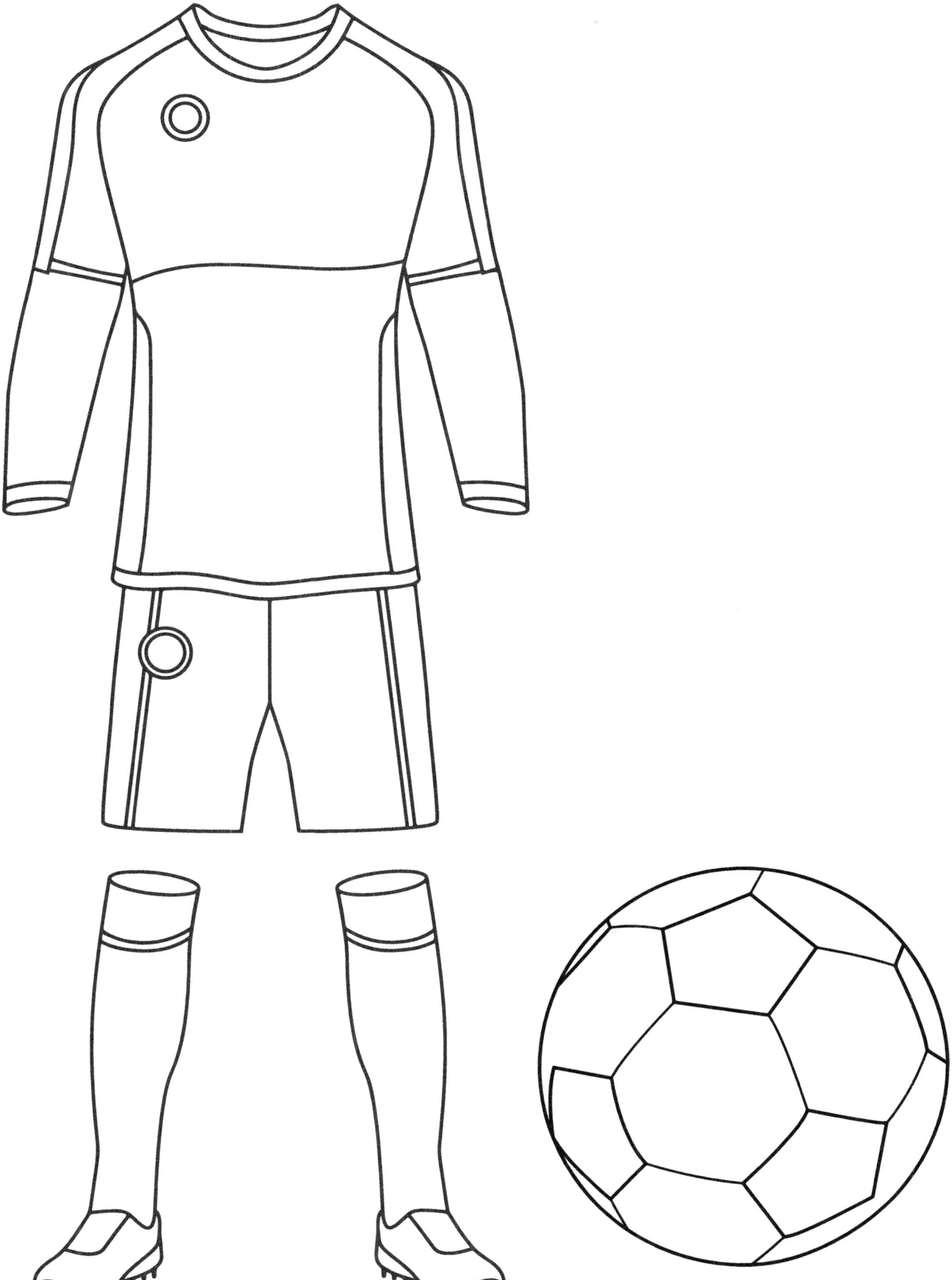

DID YOU KNOW!!

The Miracle of Leicester City: In the 2015-2016 Premier League season, Leicester City defied all odds to win the title. Starting the season with 5000-1 odds, they shocked the world by finishing first, marking one of the greatest underdog stories in sports history.

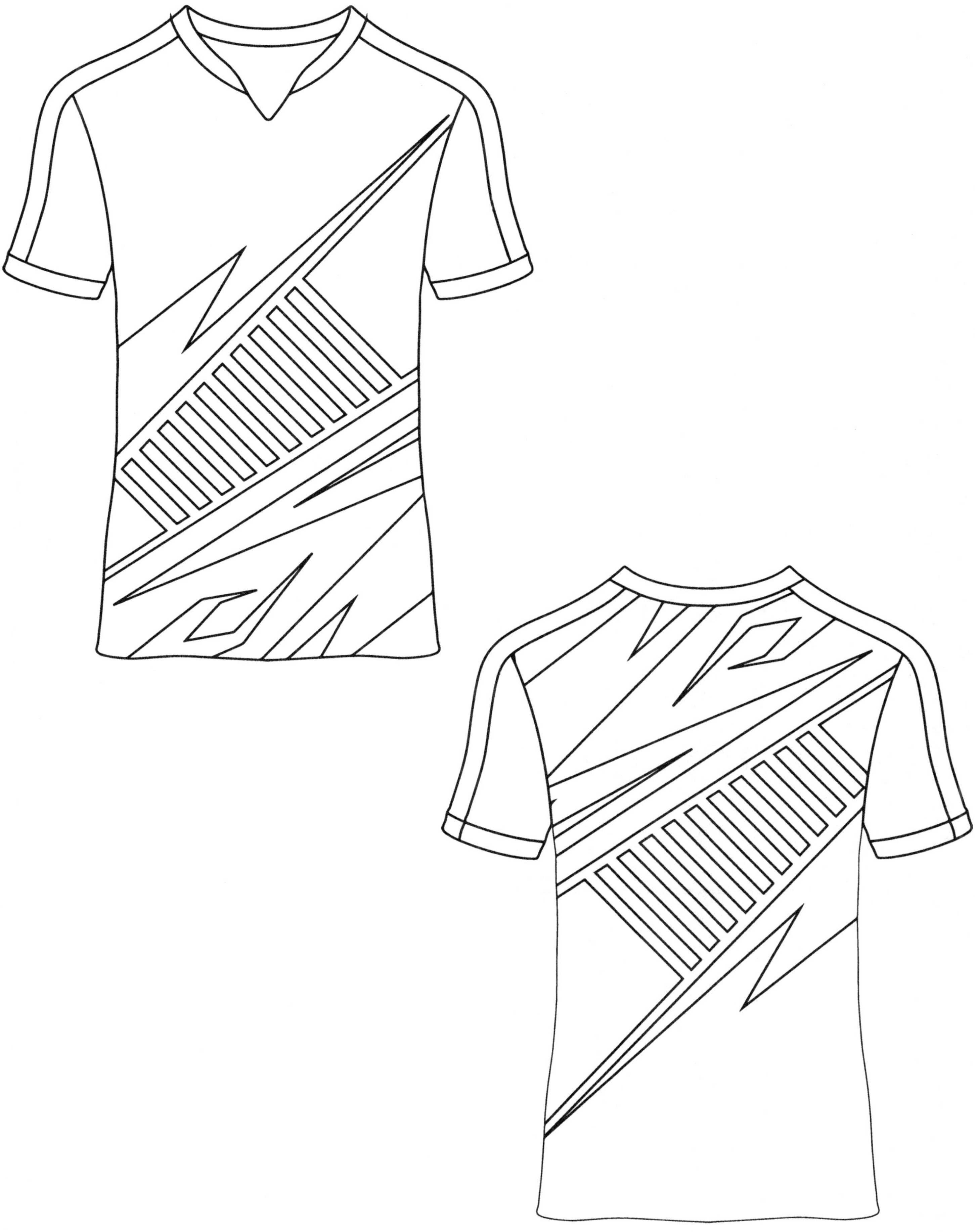

DID YOU KNOW!!

The Fastest Hat-Trick Ever: In 2015, Sadio Mané scored the fastest hat-trick in Premier League history for Southampton against Aston Villa. He scored three goals in just 2 minutes and 56 seconds, a record that still stands.

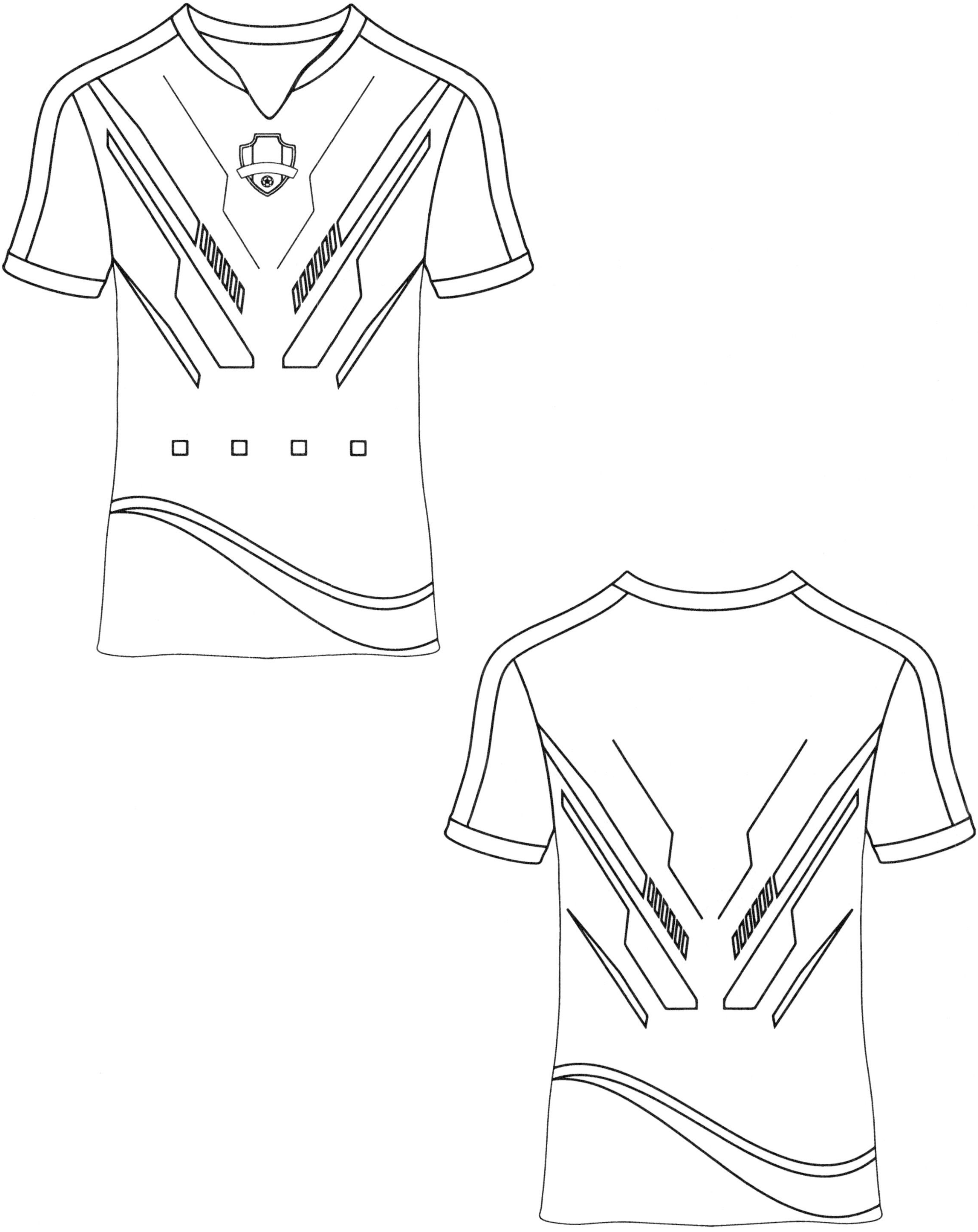

DID YOU KNOW!!

Penalty Shootout Drama: The first penalty shootout in a World Cup final occurred in 1994, when Brazil defeated Italy. The match ended in a 0-0 draw after extra time, and Brazil won 3-2 in the shootout, claiming their fourth World Cup title.

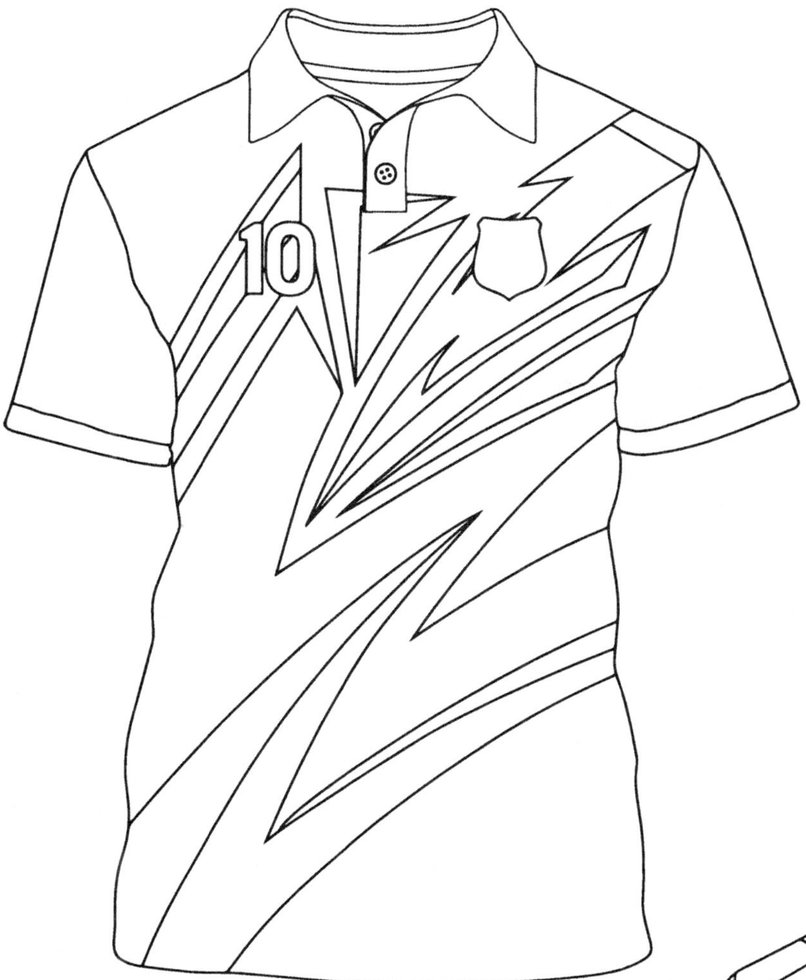
10

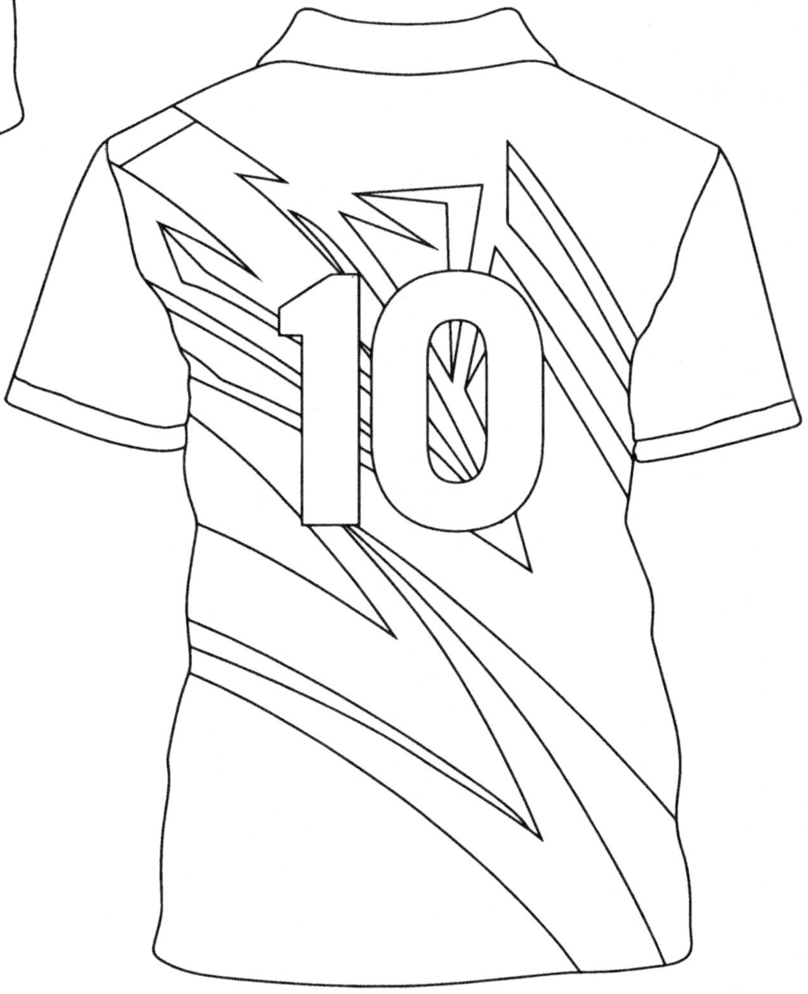
10

DID YOU KNOW!!

The Youngest World Cup Winner: Pelé, the Brazilian football legend, became the youngest player to win a World Cup at just 17 years old in 1958. He scored twice in the final against Sweden, cementing his place in football history.

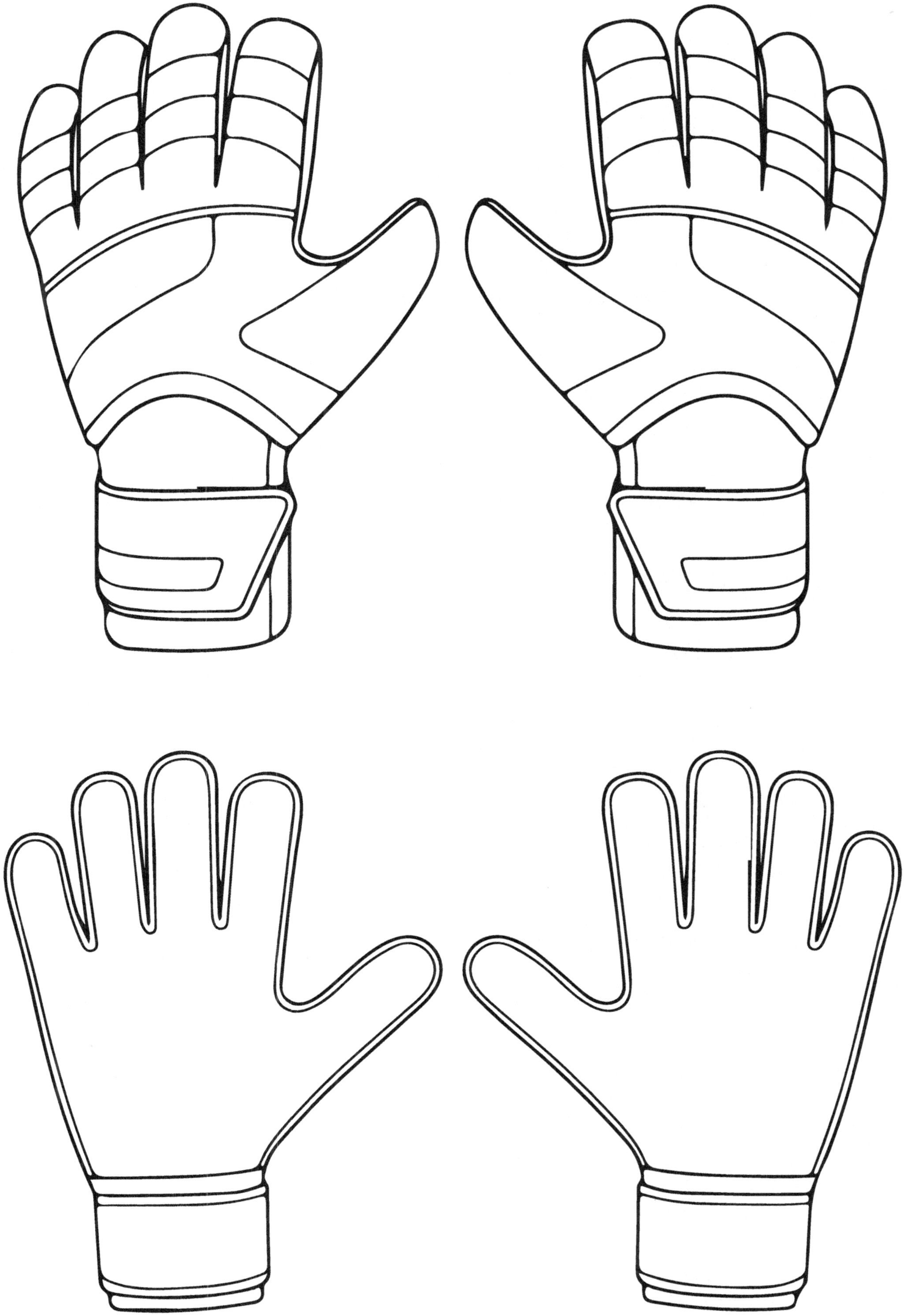

DID YOU KNOW!!

The Record for Most Goals in a Calendar Year: Lionel Messi set a record in 2012 by scoring 91 goals in a calendar year, surpassing Gerd Müller's previous record of 85 goals. Messi's incredible scoring ability has made him one of the greatest players of all time.

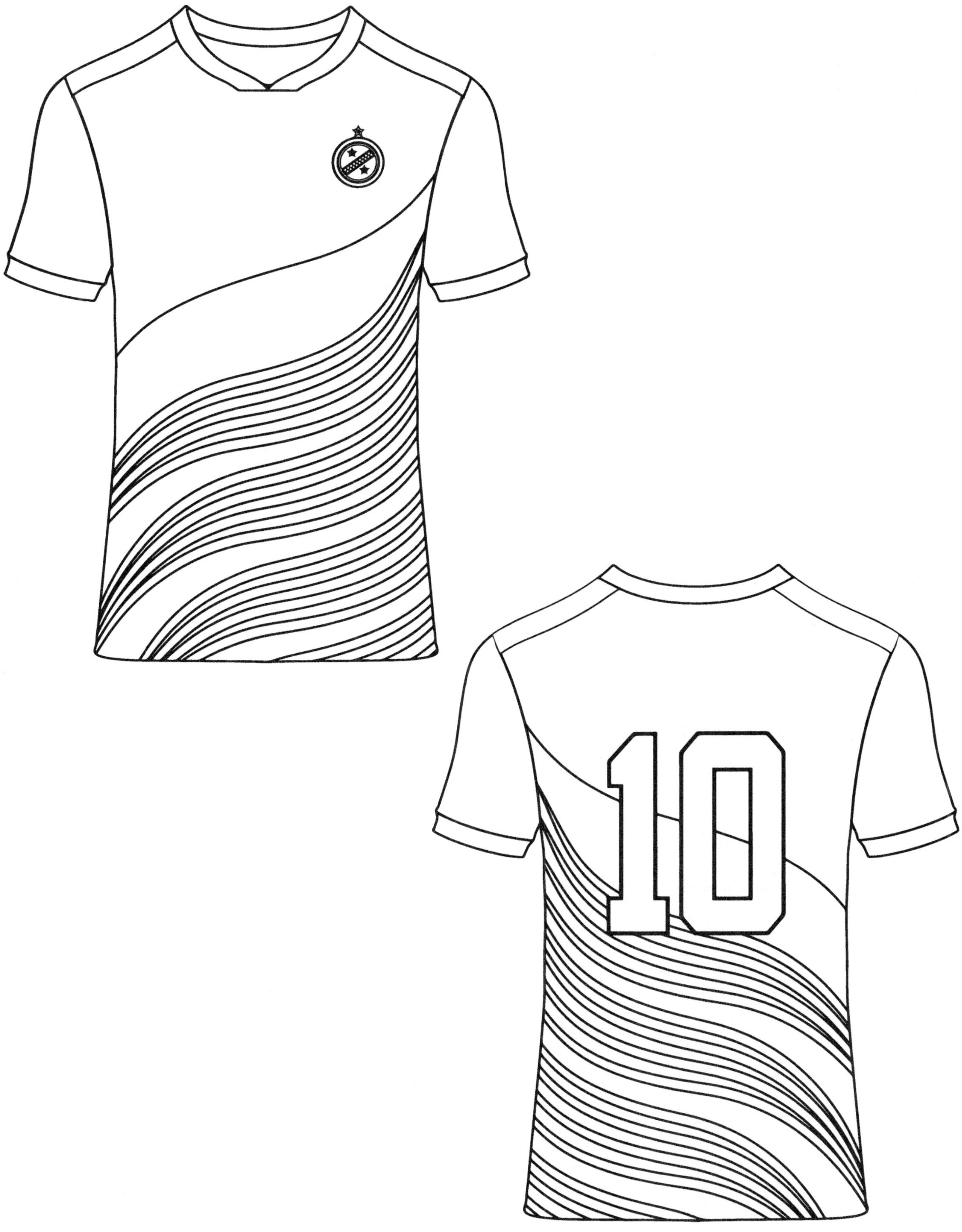
10

DID YOU KNOW!!

The First FIFA World Cup Broadcast: The 1954 FIFA World Cup in Switzerland was the first to be broadcast on television. It marked the beginning of football's rise as a global spectacle, bringing the excitement of the game to millions of homes worldwide.

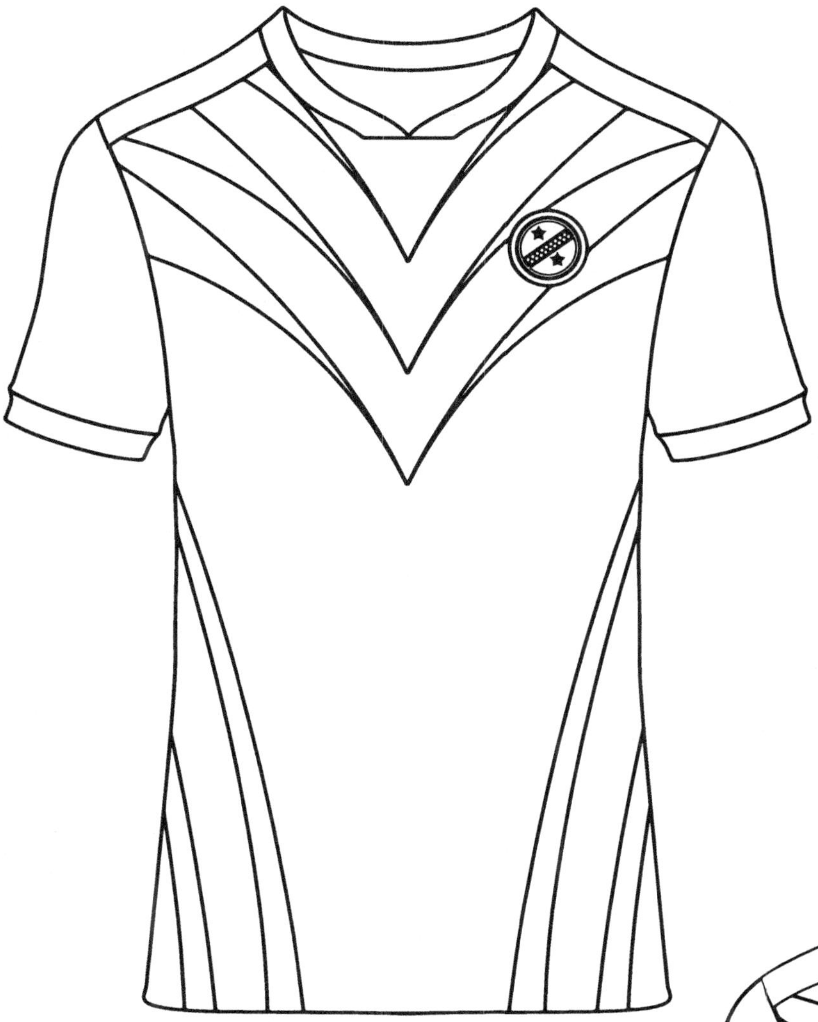

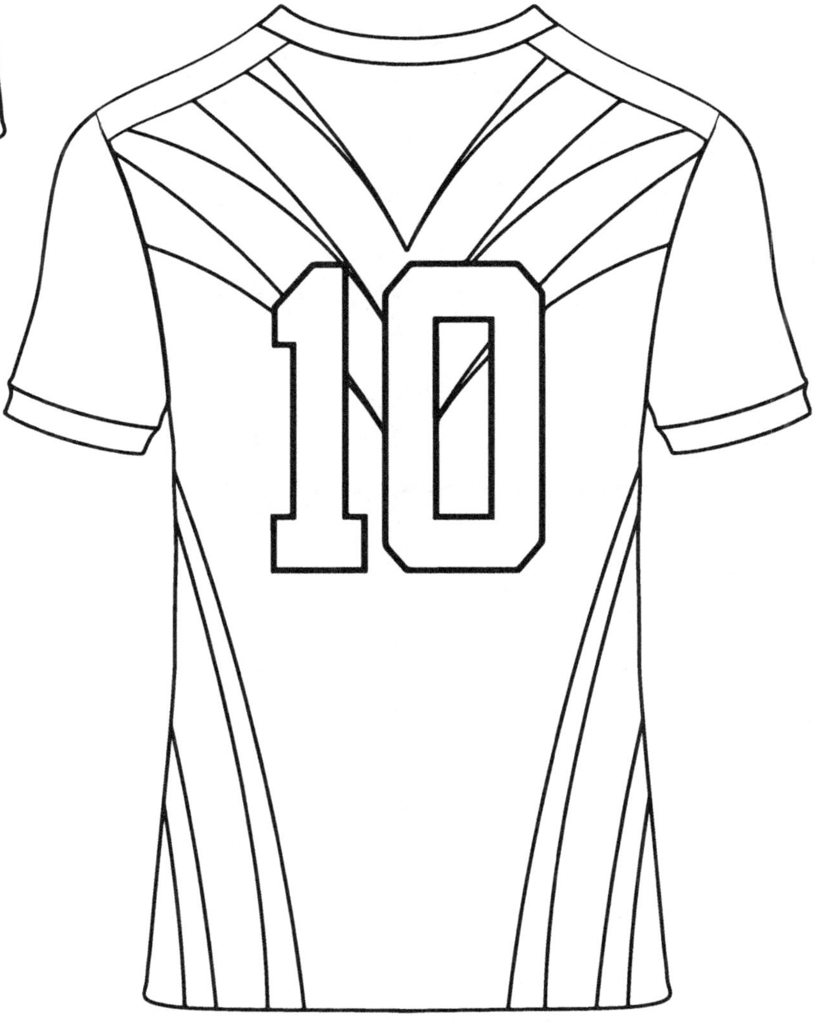
10

DID YOU KNOW!!

The Record for Most World Cup Appearances: As of 2022, Lionel Messi holds the record for the most appearances in FIFA World Cup tournaments, having played in five World Cups for Argentina from 2006 to 2022, eventually winning the title in 2022.

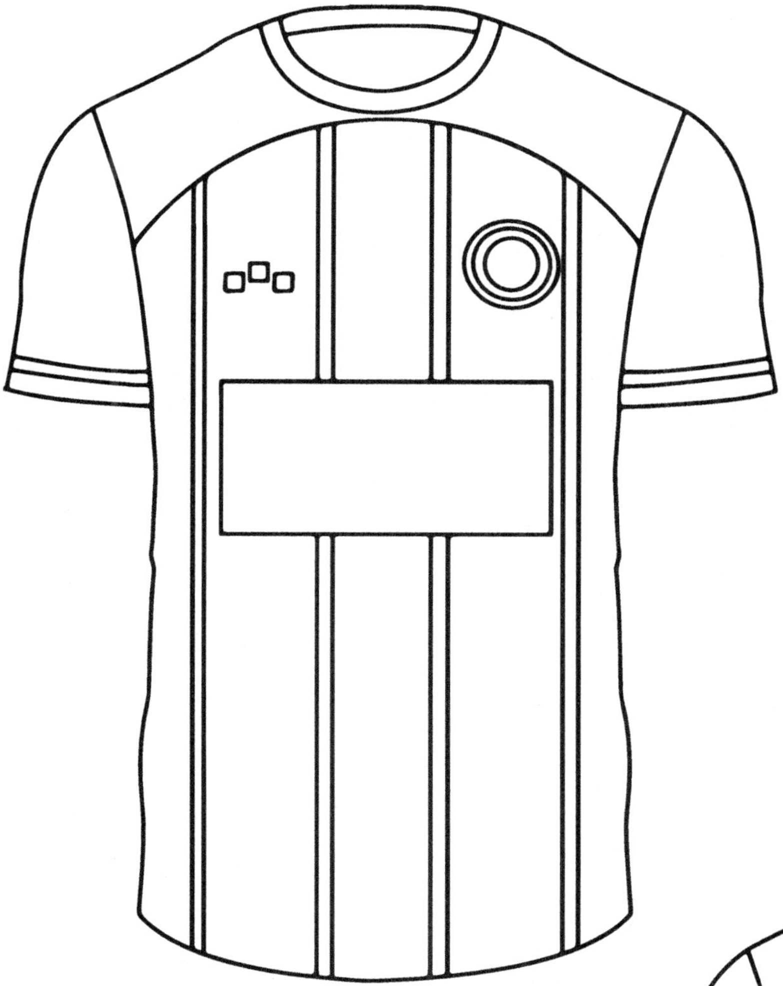

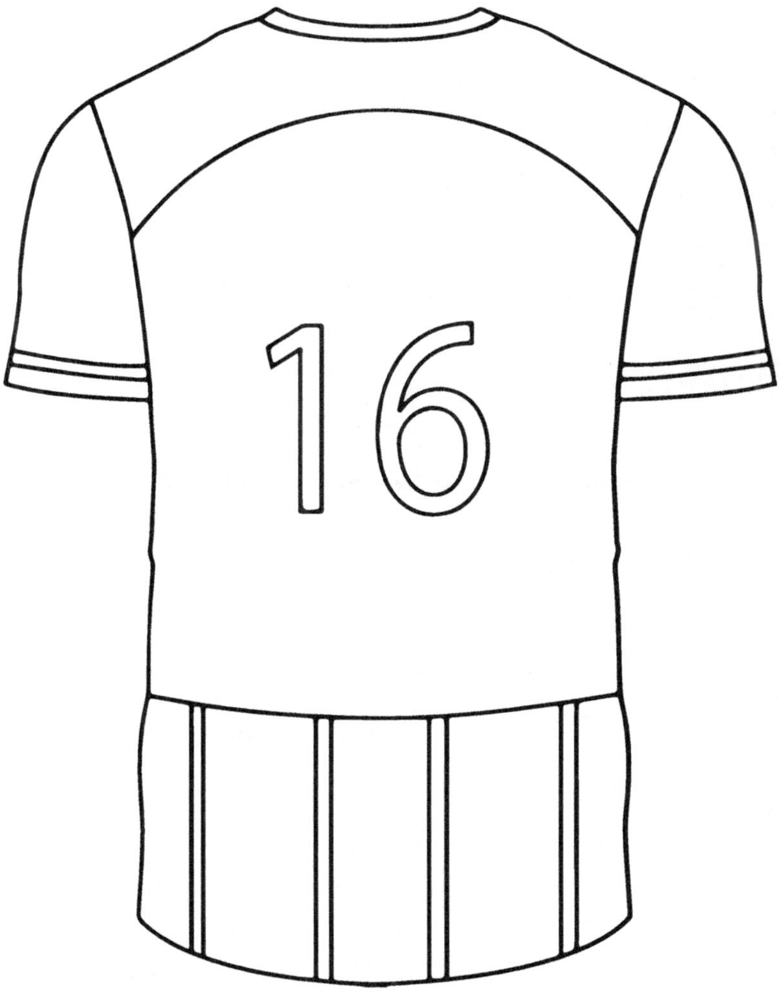
16

DID YOU KNOW!!

The First Women's Ballon d'Or Winner: In 2018, Ada Hegerberg of Norway became the first-ever recipient of the Women's Ballon d'Or, recognizing her as the best female footballer in the world. This milestone was a significant step forward for women's football.

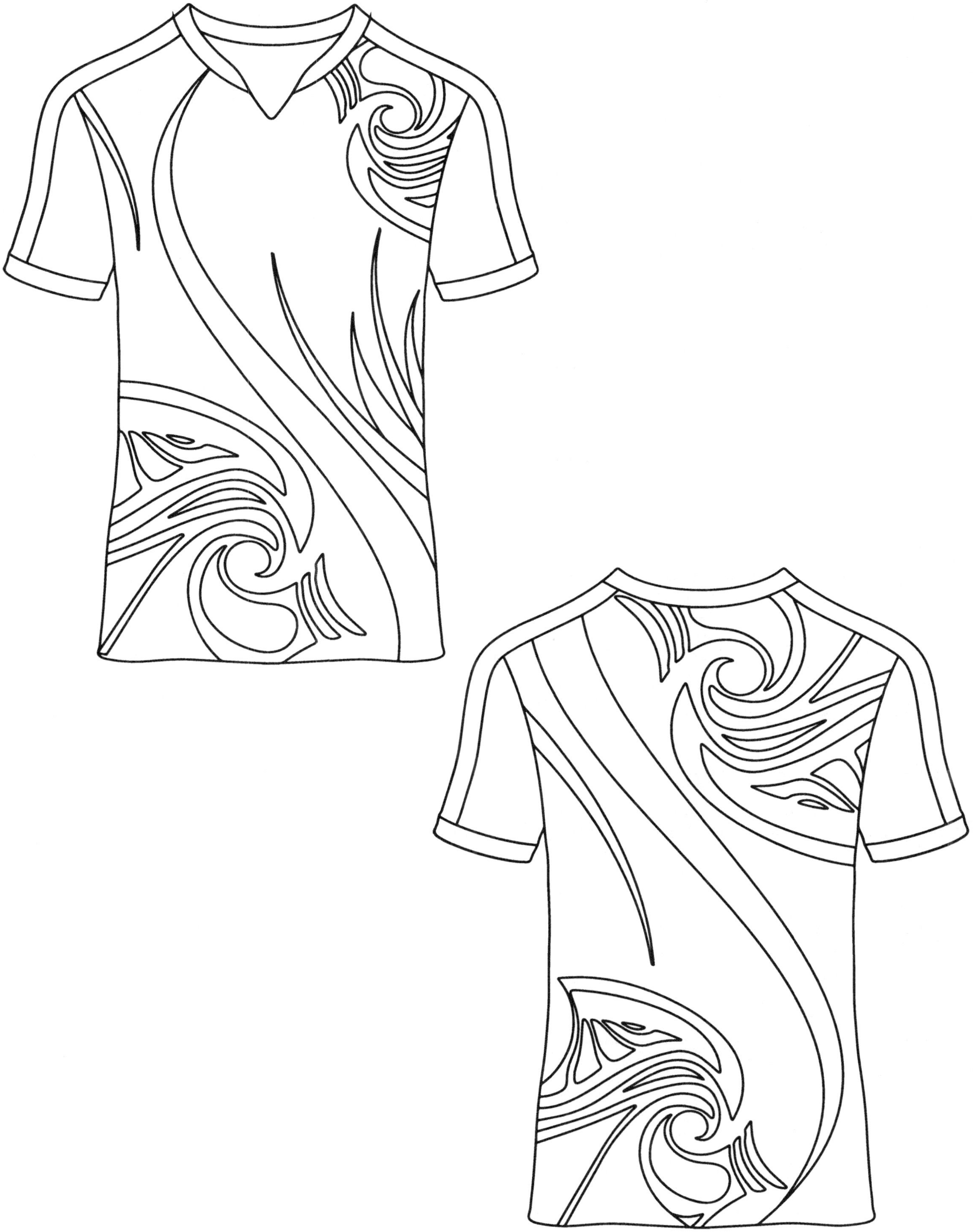

SECTION 2: DESIGN YOUR OWN FOOTBALL KIT WITH BLANK TEMPLATES

You're almost at the finish line of your football adventure! In this section, it's time for you to shine. Now that you've tried out different patterns, it's your turn to create your own football kits from scratch!

With blank templates ready for your designs, you can pick the patterns, colors, and styles that will make your team's kit totally unique. Each page is like a new, blank canvas for you to make something awesome.

As always, you'll find some fun football facts on the back of each page to keep you inspired. So, get ready to be super creative and make kits that will make your team stand out!

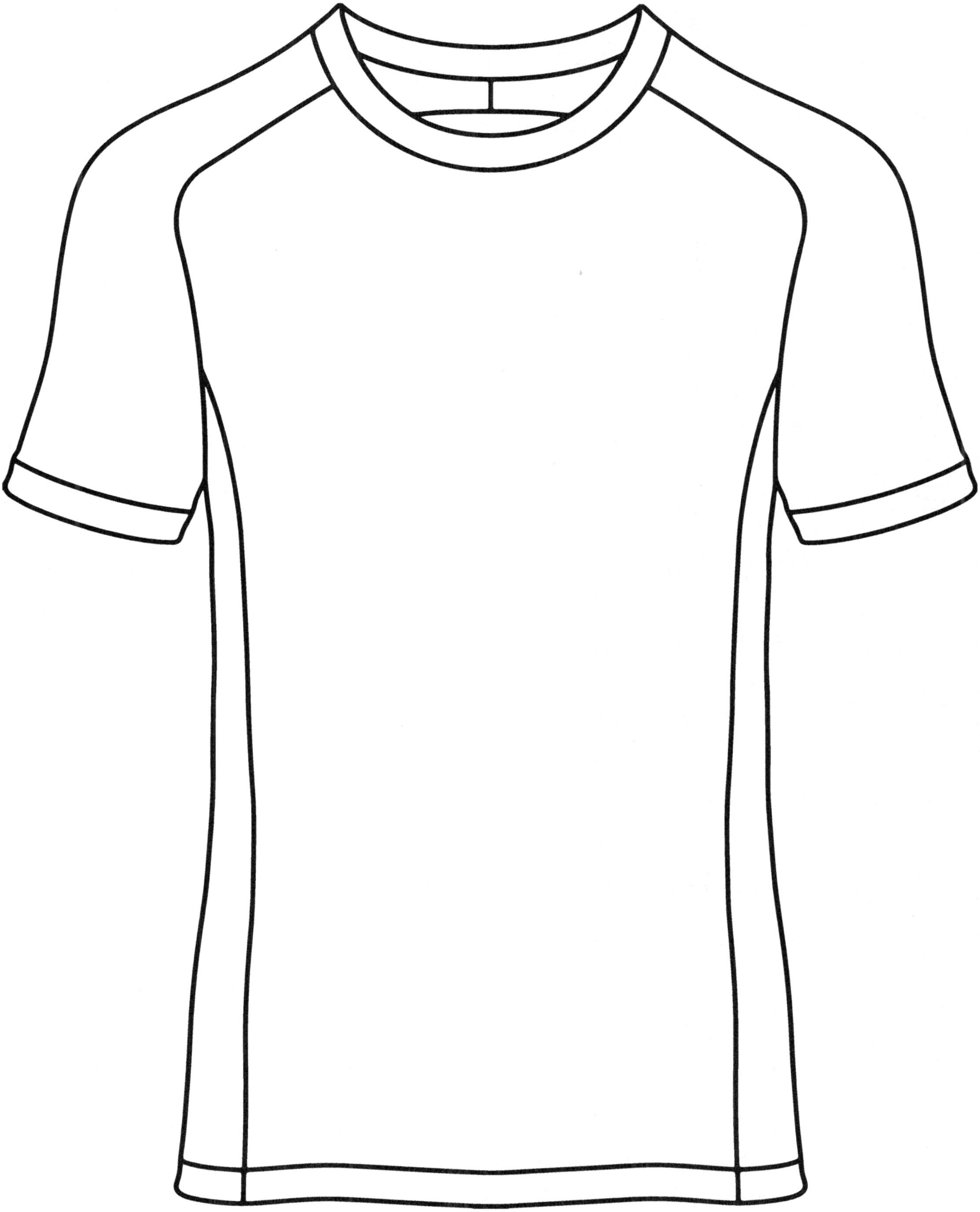

DID YOU KNOW!!

The Hand of God Goal: One of the most famous moments in football history occurred during the 1986 FIFA World Cup when Diego Maradona scored the controversial "Hand of God" goal against England. Despite using his hand, the goal was allowed, and Argentina went on to win the World Cup.

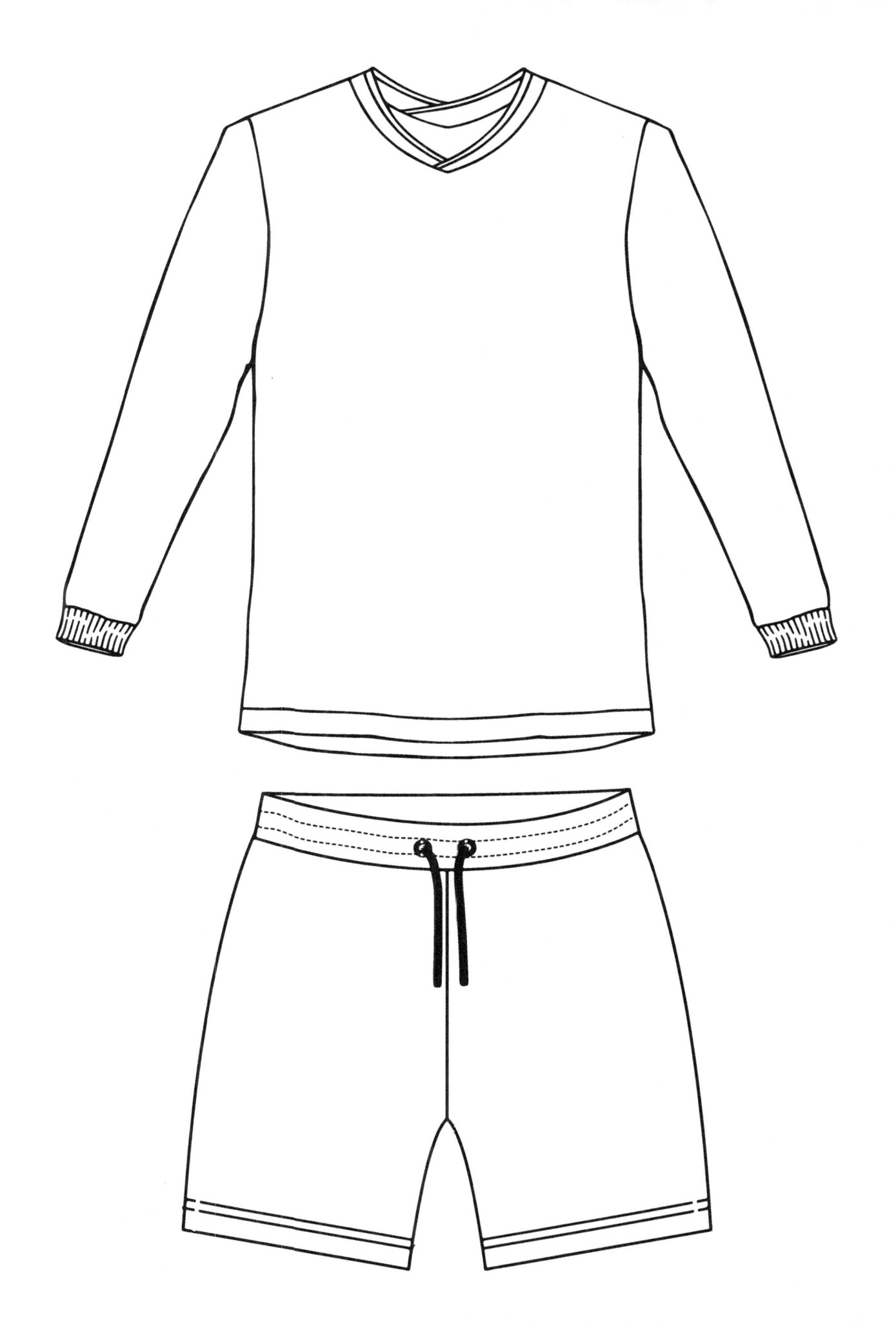

DID YOU KNOW!!

The Youngest Goalscorer in Premier League History: In 2023, Ethan Nwaneri of Arsenal became the youngest goalscorer in Premier League history at just 15 years and 181 days old. His goal marked a historic moment, highlighting the increasing presence of young talent in top-tier football.

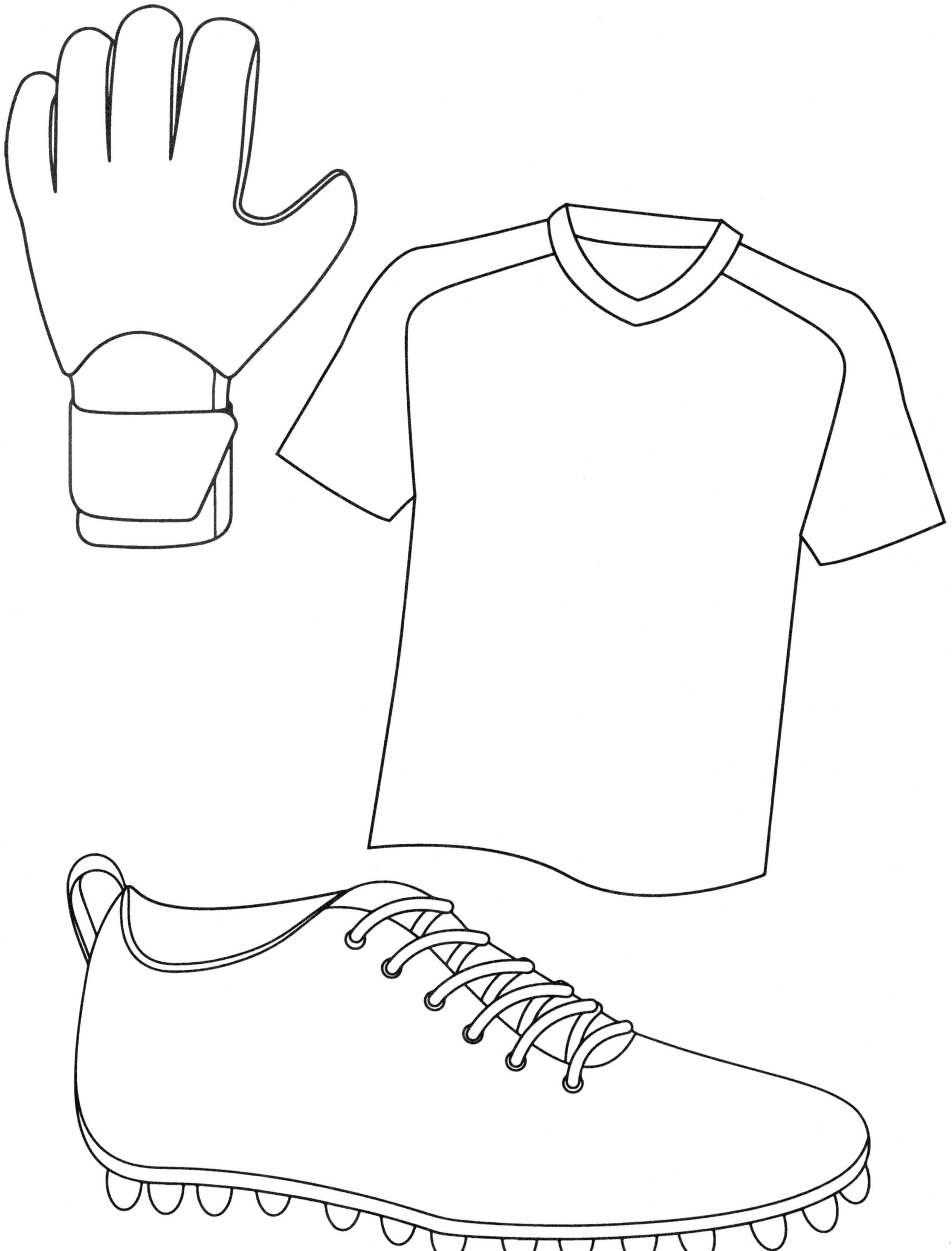

DID YOU KNOW!!

Brazil's Record 5 World Cup Wins: Brazil holds the record for the most FIFA World Cup titles, having won the tournament five times (1958, 1962, 1970, 1994, 2002). Brazil's football legacy is built on a rich history of legendary players and iconic moments.

DID YOU KNOW!!

First African Country to Host the World Cup: South Africa made history in 2010 by becoming the first African nation to host the FIFA World Cup. The tournament was a significant moment for the continent and featured memorable moments, including the introduction of the vuvuzela.

DID YOU KNOW!!

The Longest Unbeaten Run in International Football: As of 2023, Italy holds the record for the longest unbeaten run in international football, with 37 matches between 2018 and 2021. This streak included their triumph in the UEFA Euro 2020, highlighting Italy's resurgence as a footballing power.

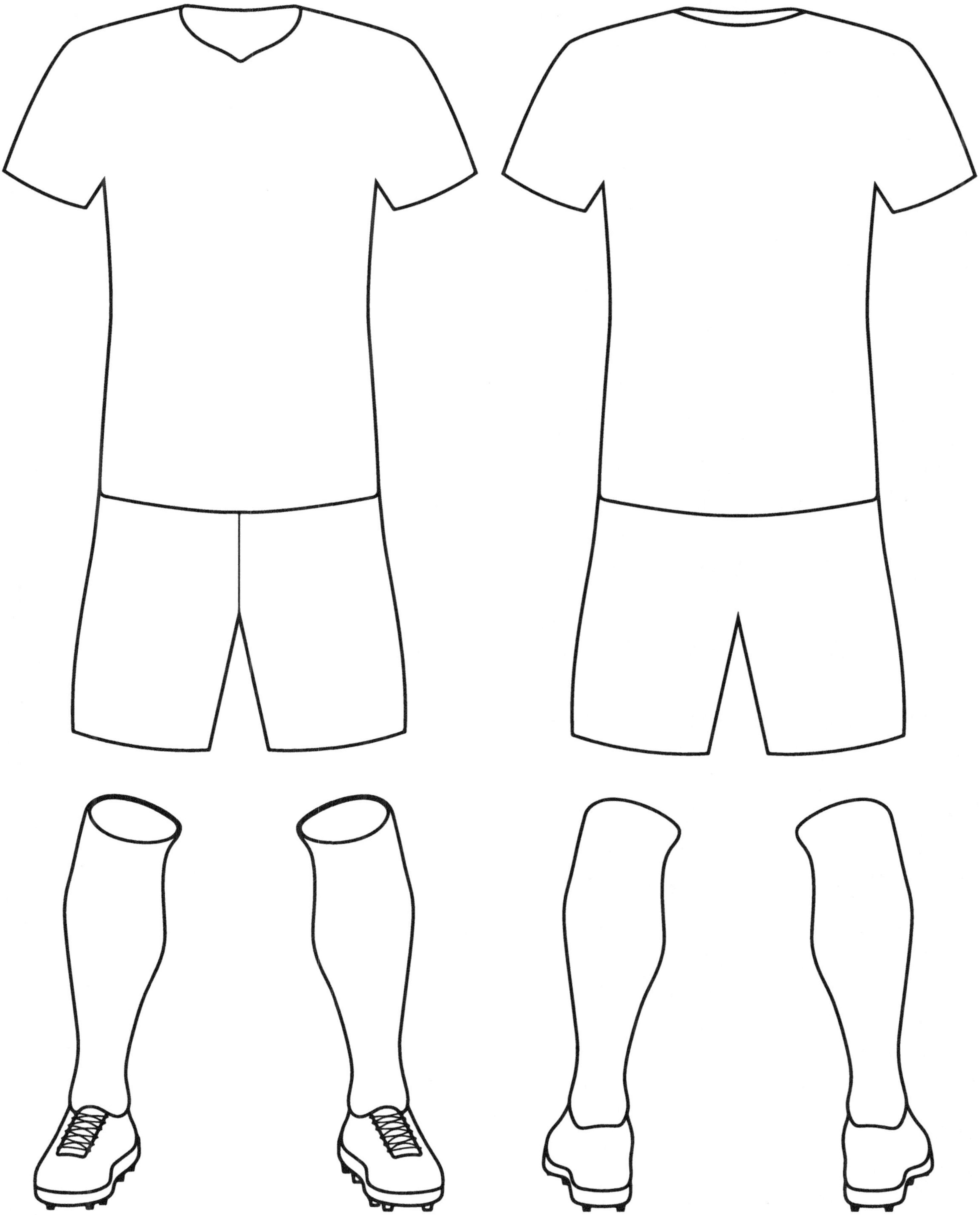

DID YOU KNOW!!

The World's Largest Football Stadium: The Rungrado 1st of May Stadium in Pyongyang, North Korea, is the largest football stadium in the world, with a seating capacity of 114,000. Despite its size, it's mostly used for large-scale performances and occasional football matches.

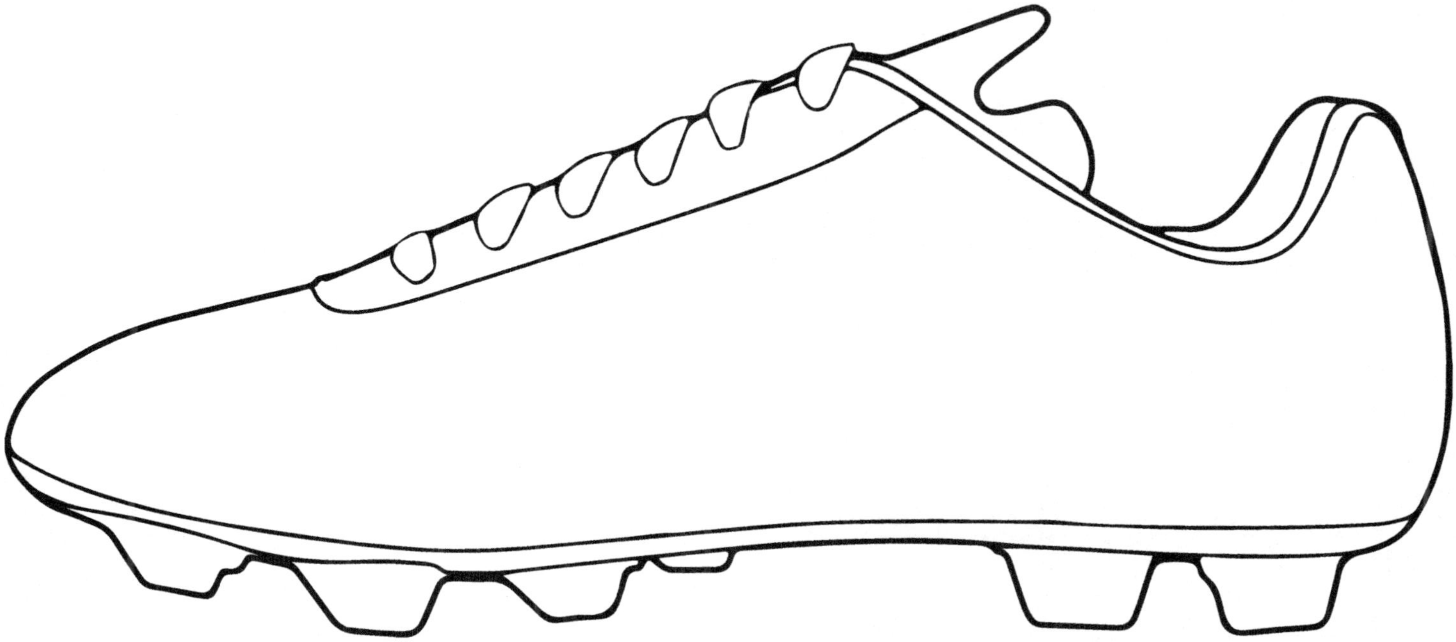

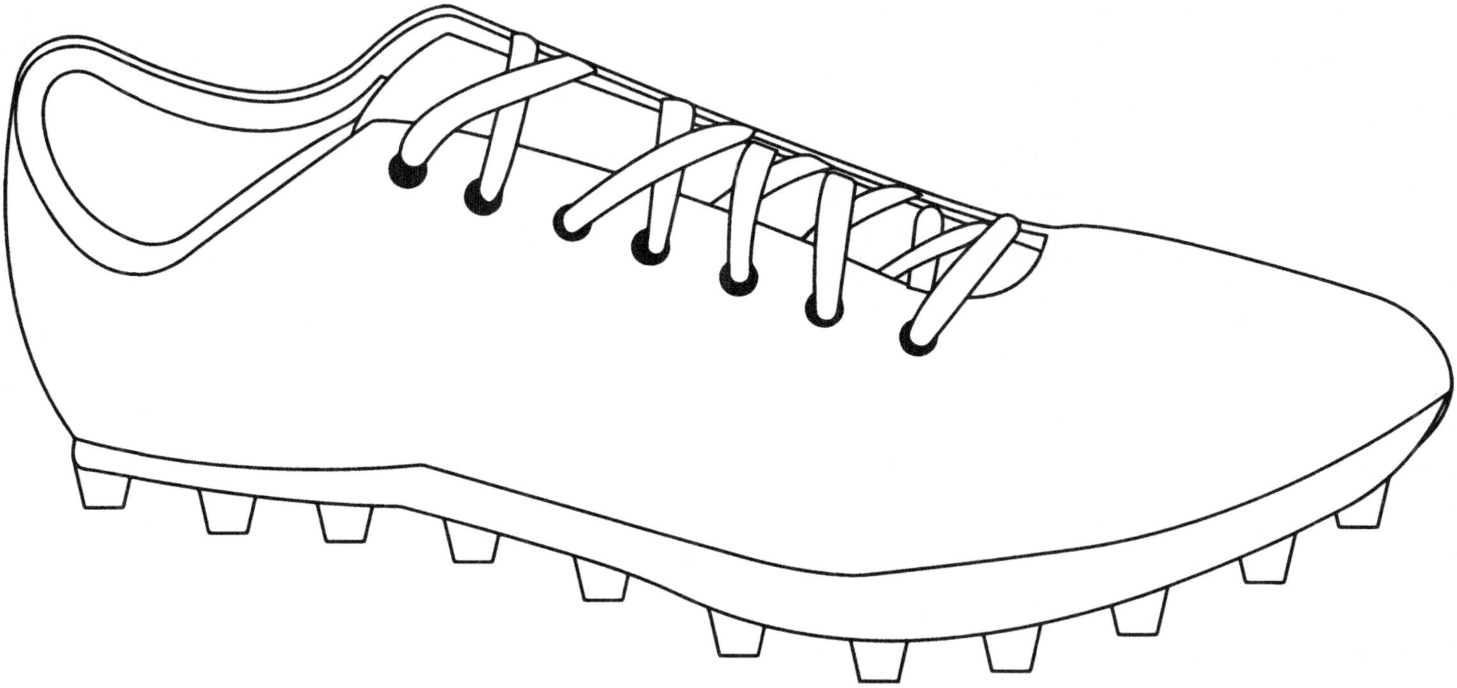

DID YOU KNOW!!

The Most Successful European Club in UEFA Competitions: Real Madrid holds the record for the most UEFA Champions League titles, with 15 victories as of 2024. Their dominance in European football is unmatched, with a legacy built on decades of success.

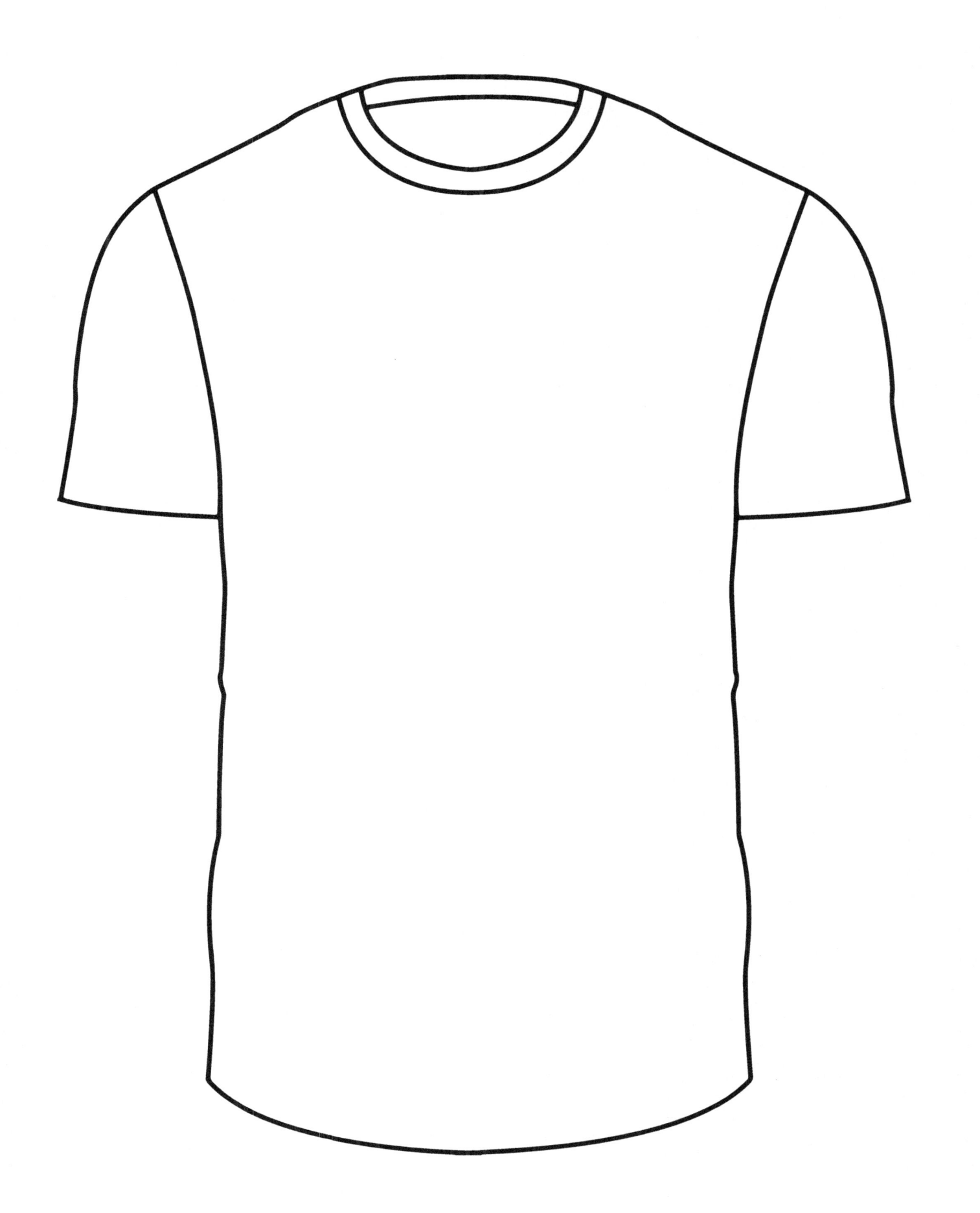

Printed in Great Britain
by Amazon